PARENTS
KIDS &
SPORTS

PARENTS KIDS & SPORTS

by

BERNIE SCHOCK

MOODY PRESS

CHICAGO

To Phil, Howard, and Gene,
who taught me how to think biblically

Library of Congress Cataloging in Publication Data

Schock, Bernie A., 1948-
    Parents, kids, and sports.

    Includes bibliographical references.
    1. Sports for children—United States.   I. Title.
GV709.2.S37   1987   796'.01'9220973   86-33330
ISBN 0-8024-6307-X

1 2 3 4 5 6 7 Printing/PC/Year 92 91 90 89 88 87

Printed in the United States of America

Contents

Introduction

My mouth was dry; my stomach was churning. It was Super Bowl Sunday, and the Dallas Cowboys had another chance to win the big game. In 1966 and 1967 the Cowboys narrowly lost championship games to Vince Lombardi's Green Bay Packers. The two following years they lost playoff games to inferior Cleveland teams. Like other Dallas fans, I agonized over their ineptitude. But redemption seemed close at hand, primarily because of the team's "Doomsday Defense." In the first two games of the playoffs the defense had allowed only ten points. In the Super Bowl they were equally impressive, stealing the ball from the Baltimore Colts seven times. But somehow the offense lost the game. I was numb for several days. Then I became angry; why was I so torn by a mere football game?

The following spring I promised my wife a day-long picnic. Foolishly, I hadn't checked the TV listings. It was the beginning of the NCAA basketball tournament. What a dreary day—even though it was sun-splashed, windless, and warm—as I pined over the missed basketball. Once again I became angry; why was I unable to enjoy that ideal day?

Those experiences and others goaded me to investigate the meaning of sports. As I examined the issues, I realized that I was not unique. Consider these facts:

- High school students were asked if they would like to be remembered as a "brilliant student," a "star athlete," or "most popular." Most chose "star athlete."[1]
- Organized sports have more than 20 million youth participants each year.[2]
- During one three-year period, girls' participation in interscholastic sports increased 350 percent.[3]
- Children overwhelmingly choose (boys, 75 percent; girls, 50 percent) physical activities over any other nonschool activities (e.g., reading or playing an instrument).[4]
- Each year 2.5 million adults volunteer to coach, officiate, and administer children's sports.[5]
- A national survey found that 77 percent of parents believe that sports can teach their children important lessons that cannot be learned in the classroom.[6]

A study of these facts led Dr. Jack Berryman of the University of Washington to conclude that sports has "become one of the most pervasive influences in the lives of

1. James Coleman, "Athletes in High Schools: A Continuing Debate," *Annals of the American Academy of Political and Social Science* 338 (1961): 38.
2. Richard Magill, Michael Ash, and Frank Smoll, eds., *Children in Sport* (Champaign, Ill.: Human Kinetics, 1982), p. xvi.
3. Thomas Shaffer, "The Young Athlete," in Magill, Ash, and Smoll, p. 119.
4. Doug Kleiber and Glyn Roberts, "The Relationship Between Game and Sport Involvement in Later Childhood," *Research Quarterly* 54, no. 2 (1983): 201.
5. Rainer Martens, ed., *Joy and Sadness in Children's Sport* (Champaign, Ill.: Human Kinetics, 1978), p. 9.
6. Tom Weir, "High School Sports Have a Place," *USA Today*, 28 Dec. 1983.

many American children."[7] But what is that influence? Why are sports so appealing? Are the majority of children helped or harmed by participation? How does our society's zeal for sports affect a child's devotion to spiritual matters? How are children affected by seemingly omnipresent athletes who endorse everything from Jesus to beer? The permeation of sports in the lives of children makes these issues critical.

But many are unwilling to examine sports seriously. No wonder. We are continually warned about the dangers of pollution, the threat of nuclear war, the hazards of food additives, and the perils of new diseases. People may say, "Please don't tell me that my leisure time is a threat to my health, too!"

One Sunday in the late 1960s President Nixon aired a political appeal at the halftime of each professional football game. Art Buchwald explained why fans were irate: "It was a blunder of colossal proportions. The silent majority will listen to anything the president has to say six days a week. But Sunday they set aside to watch football. They don't want to hear about Viet Nam, the economy, law and order or violence in the streets."[8]

But because children are adulated for their ability to score goals and scorned for their ineptitude, we must try to understand such acclaim. Because children dream about becoming the next Larry Bird or the next Chris Evert Lloyd, we must try to analyze the allure of sports. Sports are said to be changing the course of childhood, so we must overcome our aversion to examining sports critically.

7. Jack Berryman, "The Rise of Highly Organized Sports for Preadolescent Boys," in Magill, Ash, and Smoll, p. 3.
8. Larry Merchant, *And Every Day You Take Another Bite* (New York: Dell, 1971), pp. 42-43.

We often feel apprehensive about critiquing the things we love. As a young Christian, my spiritual life revolved around Campus Crusade for Christ. When I arrived at seminary, I found that not everyone shared my enthusiasm for this ministry. I was hurt and angry. How could a Christian say anything derogatory about Campus Crusade? That experience was the beginning of an important lesson for me: nothing human is above constructive criticism. "Wounds from a friend can be trusted, but an enemy multiplies kisses" (Proverbs 27:6). Even sports need loving critics who will wound when necessary. This book has been written to improve—not destroy—sports.

Part 1

Analyzing Children's Sports

1

The Strengths of Children's Sports

More than 20 million children participate in organized sports each year, and the numbers are growing. But what is the impact on the participants? Sports psychologist Terry Orlick describes the wildly divergent experiences of children:

> For every positive psychological or social outcome in sports, there are possible negative outcomes. For example, sports can offer a child group membership or group exclusion, acceptance or rejection, positive feedback or negative feedback, a sense of accomplishment or a sense of failure, evidence of self-worth or a lack of evidence of self-worth.[1]

What causes such diversity? The answer can be seen, in part, by analyzing the strengths and weaknesses of children's sports. First we will look at the strengths.

1. Terry Orlick, *Winning Through Cooperation* (Washington, D.C.: Acropolis, 1978), p. vii.

THE POTENTIAL OF SPORTS

An incensed coach attacks a referee at the conclusion of a hockey game. A parent lies about his child's age so he can compete against younger children. Enraged parents of opposing baseball teams assault each other with bats. Some psychologists warn us that organized sports are destructive to the emotional health of many children. How are we as parents to respond?

Some look only at the negative side of sports and conclude that they should be abandoned. We sometimes forget that good things are often abused. I do not want to forfeit my marriage because there are many bad marriages. I do not want to abstain from eating because many people overeat. And I do not think that sports must be discarded simply because there are people who abuse them. Sports are a gift from God that can be used—or abused. When used properly, they offer enduring benefits to children.

PHYSICAL DEVELOPMENT

"Johnny, would you please mow the lawn this afternoon?"

"Dad, why do *I* always have to do it? Why don't you ask Mary once in a while?"

"I do ask her to help. But I'm asking *you* this time."

"But, Dad, you always make me do more."

Ask a child to mow the lawn or clean his room, and he may think that you've asked him to perform a Herculean task. But allow him onto a basketball court, and he has the energy to play for hours. Competitive games are a pleasurable way for kids to exercise.

Exercise makes an important contribution to physical health. Wilbert Leonard describes some of the benefits of exercise:

Exercise that accompanies some sports may not only firm up the muscles and make the body look good, but it can also bring about positive changes in the cardiovascular system, reduce cholesterol and triglyceride levels in the blood, produce weight loss through caloric consumption, reduce blood pressure readings, and reapportion body fat.[2]

But physical gains quickly fade. Like eating, exercise must be continued if physical health is to be maintained. Thus, it is the *habit* of exercise that we want to instill in our children. No amount of exercise in childhood will be sufficient to support physical health as an adult.

EMOTIONAL DEVELOPMENT

"Watch out, batter! Here comes his high, hard one."
"Hey, batter, this guy knocked a guy out last week."
"Here it comes! Here it comes! Watch out! Duck!"
Children's merciless badgering of opposing hitters has one goal: to scare the daylights out of them. Children in sports are confronted with a host of negative emotions: worry over performance, fear of getting hit with a baseball or being tackled too hard, discouragement when their team loses, anger over a referee's decision. Fortunately such emotions are usually washed away by other games and other seasons. However, later in life disappointments won't be so easily laundered. For example, the judgment of a man's boss may limit that man's lifelong opportunities for advancement. Sports provide opportunities for children to experiment with emotions without suffering crushing consequences.

Furthermore, exercise can work as an antidote to

2. Wilbert M. Leonard II, *A Sociological Perspective of Sport* (Minneapolis: Burgess, 1980), p. 71.

depression and tension. A regular jogging program for emotionally disturbed boys made them more outgoing and emotionally stable than a control group of disturbed boys.[3] Another study determined that a fifteen minute walk was just as effective as a tranquilizer in reducing tension. Grade school teachers have long recognized that a fifteen minute "tranquilizer" called recess is effective in reducing stress in children.

Finally, sports may bolster children's emotional lives by communicating that it is OK to have fun. Sports are not all negative emotions; if they were, few would participate. Many summer mornings during my youth I rode the bus across town to play sandlot baseball with my cousins and their friends. My mom was astonished at how early I would get up to play ball. I didn't want to risk arriving late for choosing teams. We spent the whole morning playing, stopped for lunch, and went swimming in the afternoon. Reminiscing, I find that I am one of those "numberless American males [who] cling as long as life and common sense will let them to the days when a game of baseball could fill a whole hot afternoon so full that it would run over at the edges."[4]

Some of us have a tendency to work too hard, take life too seriously, and be too responsible. When Paul wrote to Timothy he gave instructions on the proper use of money. Although greed was to be discouraged and generosity encouraged, Timothy was also to remind them that God "richly provides us with everything for our enjoyment" (1 Timothy 6:17). Money, as well as other gifts such as friends, family, time, gardens, and games, is given, in part, for our pleasure.

3. H. Dulberg and F. Bennet, "Psychological Changes in Adolescent Males Induced by Systematic Exercise," *American Corrective Therapy Journal* 34, no. 5 (1980): 142.
4. Richard Lipsky, *How We Play the Game* (Boston: Beacon, 1981), p. 76.

INTELLECTUAL DEVELOPMENT

During my seminary days, whenever I had trouble concentrating while studying, I would stop for some strenuous exercise. It seemed more effective than caffeine in keeping me alert. In fact, it was so effective that it created the opposite problem—insomnia!

Exercise plays an important role in helping us use our minds to their fullest. Research has found that exercise retards the normal decline of mental functioning in the elderly.[5] Physical fitness improves a person's ability to learn, whatever his innate capability.

SOCIAL DEVELOPMENT

A group of children gather to play football. Last week the third graders bullied the second graders into age-divided teams. The obvious outcome made the younger group adamant: this time they will not play unless there is a more equitable division. They are learning a lesson in fairness. A discussion of the rules follows. The bigger kids argue for tackle; the smaller ones insist on touch. This is a lesson in sensitivity to the capabilities of others. As the game progresses, a number of conflicts arise: "I touched you!" "No you didn't!" "Yes I did!" The kids are learning yet another lesson, this one on the resolution of conflicts. A little later, one of the uncoordinated boys decides to quit. He is tired of hiking the ball on every play. But wait, he owns the football! His team recognizes his inestimable worth and lets him play quarterback. The children are learning how to be gracious. Potentially, sports can teach kids how to get along with others.

Furthermore, many athletes have formed special re-

---

5. R. Young, "The Effect of Regular Exercise on Cognitive Functioning and Personality," *British Journal of Sports Medicine* 13 (1979): 110.

lationships in sports. When I was a sophomore in a large high school, I tried out for the basketball team. The first day the gym was crammed with 120 teenage boys. Only 15 would make the "A" squad and 15 the "B" squad. On recommendations from junior high coaches, the group was divided into two groups of 60. I despaired when I found myself among the soon-to-be-cut boys. We were hurried through a couple of drills—more out of courtesy than as a test of our skills—before being banished. But the coach of the "B" squad, Mr. Newcombe, saw something in me. Though he screamed constantly—and often solely—at me, I loved him. I knew that he was laboring to make me a better player. As a result of his teaching and his confidence in me, I not only made the "B" squad but by the end of the year was promoted to the "A" squad. I will always have fond memories of that coach.

PSYCHOLOGICAL DEVELOPMENT

Christian psychologist Larry Crabb contends that to be psychologically sound, people need significance and security.

Significance. Our two oldest sons both enjoy competitive games. But when they compete against each other, the younger, Andrew, is the predictable loser. Recently, though, I have seen that he has formed a strategy for coping with the situation. He has concentrated on mastering a few skills so that he can beat his brother at something. One activity he has labored over is his ability to play a pinball machine at his grandparents' home. The other day I asked him, "Andrew, why are you so much better than your brother is at pinball?" A big smile spread across his face, and he said, "Because I practice!"

Every child needs to feel that he is uniquely good at

something—whether it is playing a musical instrument, hitting a tennis ball, or drawing a picture. Success in sports can give children an I-can-do-it attitude toward other challenges. People are faced with formidable tasks all through life—in school, in marriage, in work, in their walk with God. A former major league player, who had one great season and then nothing but trouble later, told how that one achievement sustained him: "How could I forget that super season? It was the only thing I had for so many years."[6] The memory of his one success became the foundation for mending his life.

Security. Over the past years I have had a growing sense of security in my marriage. With God's help, I have become more adept at sensing when my wife is upset about something—she no longer has to slam doors or bang dishes to get my attention! I have become better at planning time for us to be alone. I can even occasionally admit that I am wrong! Even so, I still act like a punished puppy when criticized. I am about as neat as a tornado. And I have a tendency to be overbearing. But even with such faults, I have no thought of her ever rejecting me. I feel secure because I know she accepts me as I am. Significance is built on accomplishment. But perfect accomplishment is a fantasy. To feel secure I need to know that I am loved and accepted even though I frequently falter.

Similarly, success in sports may contribute to your child's feelings of significance. But failure is inevitable—he won't always hit a home run or have the fastest time in a race. Failure in sports can be a primer for failure in life. If your child feels loved and accepted in spite of his shortcomings, he will feel secure.

6. Cited in *Where Have You Gone Vince Dimaggio?* by Ed Kiersh (New York: Bantam, 1983), p. 18.

Former black major league pitcher "Mudcat" Grant believed that his problems in sports trained him for life out of sports: "The racial problems, the inner struggles, they don't matter anymore. The game was a great vehicle to the future. . . . Mental defeats and heartaches have to be overcome all the time in this world, and baseball taught me how."[7] We are never as capable as we would like to be. Failure in sports may prepare kids for the realities of life.

SKILL DEVELOPMENT

Households through the centuries have echoed with children pleading, "Let me do it myself!" As children strive to master their bodies, their speech is saturated with phrases such as: "Look, Mommy, how fast I can run . . . how high I can jump . . . how far I can throw . . . how hard I can kick . . . how high I can climb." Mastering a skill is a special experience for all children regardless of their ability. Consider this observation of a handicapped boy as he competed in the Special Olympics:

> I saw a little boy stand for minutes, his eyes on the ground, sucking his finger, while two judges tried to convince him to make a try in the standing broad jump. Finally he made a token half-effort, hopping a few inches. He looked for approval and was applauded and hugged. He clasped his hands and laughed. And he jumped again. And again. And again. They could not get him to stop. Only a game of work-up among the angels could have been any happier.[8]

7. Ibid., p. 95.
8. Gary Warner, *Competition* (Elgin, Ill.: David C. Cook, 1979), p. 109.

Maybe you've witnessed the toothy grin of a child .
who has just learned how to ride a bike. Or the delight of
a child finally making contact between bat and ball.
Sports offer kids the chance to develop physical skills.
And as I mentioned, such accomplishment can give them
confidence to approach other challenges.

The development of sports skills is also significant
because athletic ability is a principal factor in gaining
peer acceptance. That may be especially important for
Christian youth who may feel like outcasts because of
their moral and spiritual commitments. But through
sports they find an acceptable way to gain the admiration
of others.

Similarly, sports can be the basis for such approval
among later maturing girls:

> In contrast to the sports enjoyed by males, women's
> sports are not so dependent on muscle strength and
> body weight. Thus, the late-maturing girl whose jeans
> and T-shirt can't be filled out nearly as well as her
> classmates' may very well be able to run faster, jump
> higher, and throw a ball better. In the past the very tall,
> late-maturing junior and senior high school girl often
> had less access to the mainstream of the most popular
> school activities. Women's basketball and volleyball
> have provided an especially welcome haven for the
> very tall adolescent who will almost always be a late
> maturer.[9]

Finally, when children cultivate their physical skills,
it creates an enduring commitment to sports and exercise. As I mentioned, because of the lifelong benefits of
exercise, it is important to develop a positive attitude to-

9. Ronald E. Smith and Frank L. Smoll, *Kidsports: A Survival Guide for Parents*
(Reading, Mass.: Addison-Wesley, 1983), p. 153.

ward physical activity in our young children. As children develop their physical abilities through sports, it may encourage them to be involved in exercise throughout their lifetimes.

MORAL DEVELOPMENT

Your team is battling for the championship. The team isn't composed of the gifted athletes that make championships common. The kids have toiled and tussled and somehow won often enough to contend for the crown. It is the final period, the game is tied, and you discover that your worst player has not played the required amount. What will you do?

Or, you are a teenage boy who believes in telling the truth, but at the crux of a football game you know that you trapped an attempted catch. Will you confess the trap or try to persuade the referee that the ball did not hit the ground? Competitive games force children, parents, and coaches to make moral choices.

But as *Sports Illustrated* writer Frank Deford said, we sometimes encourage kids to make immoral choices:

> When I was in high school we had this big center about 6-7. In one game we're down by a point with a minute to go. In a melee he's whistled for his fifth foul. Instantly, I shoot up my hand and stomp around and carry on a great act. They give me the foul, he stays in the game, and we win. I wouldn't steal anything at a store but I stole a foul. After the game the coach congratulated me, saying it was the shrewdest bit of quick thinking he'd ever seen. Off the court I would not have done the same in an equivalent situation. But on the court something immoral and unethical becomes "shrewd play."[10]

10. Frank Deford, "Would You Buy a Used Sports Illustrated from This Man?" *The Christian Athlete* 21, no. 4 (1977): 18.

Plato believed that he could uncover a person's values more effectively in an hour of play than he could in a year of conversation. Though our children's most important moral choices are future (Will they follow their peer group and experiment with drugs and sex? Will they cheat to make good grades? Will they marry someone who loves Christ?), their behavior on the athletic field may indicate the direction of those commitments. As Heywood Hale Broun has said, "Sports do not build character. They reveal it."[11]

CONCLUSION

No one can deny that there are major abuses in sports today. Some would have us abandon competitive sports and choose alternative forms of leisure. That is not only unrealistic—who is going to convince the 20 million participants and their parents that sports are bad?—but it is also unwise. Many children's sports in America may be corrupt, but they shouldn't be left to the corrupters. Jesus told us that we are the salt of the earth. Just as salt keeps food from becoming rancid, parents who care about preserving sports for children can make sports an important and satisfying experience for them.

11. James Michener, *Sports in America* (New York: Random, 1976), p. 16.

2

Sports' Inherited Weaknesses

It has been said that the church has too many unloving critics and too many uncritical lovers. Frequently our criticism of sports falls into one extreme or the other —tearing down with no concern for what remains or blindly participating with no concern for sports' abuses. Loving critics can improve the opportunities for children in sports.

There are two categories of problems that negate the benefits of sports—inherited and inherent problems. Some negative aspects of sports have been inherited from our culture. Although similar emphases are found in other cultures, they aren't found universally. Those appendages can and should be removed. On the other hand, there are problems that are inherent to competitive games. These can't be changed and still call the games competitive. They can only be watched and controlled. First we will look at the inherited problems.

An Overemphasis on Winning

I recently spoke to a service club on the subject of children and sports. At the meeting a man was given an award for not missing the weekly meeting for seventeen years. (My calculator informed me that was 884 straight meetings!) But think—what did that man sacrifice to receive such an accolade? Was he ever able to relax on an extended vacation? Was he occasionally forced to break off a conversation with a needy employee? Did his commitment make it impossible to go on a father-son canoe trip? Did he miss seminars that would have made him more effective in his job? It seems inconceivable that he hadn't occasionally ignored important needs in order to achieve such an accomplishment.

In any endeavor there are two elements: the process and the product. The service club award was given solely for a product—perfect attendance. It said nothing about the process—the obstacles he overcame to receive the award. In our culture we often glorify the accomplishment and ignore how it was accomplished. During the 1970s, the Philadelphia Flyers were the winningest hockey team in the National Hockey League. Part of the reason for their success was their intimidating style of play. That didn't matter to NHL president John Ziegler, who praised their achievement: "The Flyers are the top draw in the league. People pay money to see them. If other teams were as successful, I'd be pleased, regardless of how they achieve success."[1] The world says success is what is important; it doesn't matter how that success is achieved.

Children are often untarnished by the emphasis on winning. A couple of years ago while watching a baseball

---

1. Bob Abel and Mike Valenti, *Sports Quotes: The Inside View of the Sports World* (New York: Facts on File, 1983), p. 24.

game, one of my sons showed how naive children can be about sports. When the baseball game we were watching ended in the top of the ninth inning, he asked why they didn't play the last half. I thought it was obvious but explained that since the home team was ahead, they would win the game whether they batted or not. He got a funny look on his face and said, "So what?" He thought the home team would feel cheated because they didn't get to bat as many times as the losing team. For him, the fun was paramount; winning was secondary.

Studies have found that winning is one of the least important reasons kids give for playing sports. They play:[2]

1. to have fun
2. to improve their skills and learn new skills
3. to be with their friends or make new friends
4. for thrills and excitement
5. to become physically fit
6. to succeed or win

Because of the pervasiveness of the winning-is-everything attitude, it is important to understand the consequences of such an emphasis.

ABUSE OF PEOPLE

Abuse is displayed in various ways when winning is enthroned. First, it can incite hostility between opponents. Muzafer Sherif conducted a study of the effects of competition at a camp for boys. When the boys were divided into rival groups and awards were promised to the winners, animosity was aroused between the boys:

2. Ronald E. Smith and Frank L. Smoll, *Kidsports: A Survival Guide for Parents* (Reading, Mass.: Addison-Wesley, 1983), p. 10.

Although the games started in the spirit of good sportsmanship, as the tournament progressed this soon changed to hostility and ill will. Members of opposing teams began to call their opponents derogatory names and subsequently refused to have anything to do with them. Name calling, shoving and scuffles between rival group members extended outside the games and became the norm in the camp.[3]

Parents also maltreat their children in attempts to produce "winners." Dr. Lyle Michaeli, chairman of the sports medicine program at Children's Hospital in Boston, has found a disturbing number of mothers of young gymnasts who are practically starving their daughters of food "so that their bodies will remain immature and thus better suited to the sport."[4]

Furthermore, a coach tuned only to winning may in jure his players. Gary Shaw, a football player at the University of Texas during the mid-1960s, explained that inducing unproductive players to relinquish their scholarships was a prime ingredient in Texas's success. Obviously that was not easy; something drastic was needed. Coaches designed special drills for practice sessions. One tackling drill used as many as four men to attack a stationary ball carrier from different directions. The tacklers were sometimes sent in quick succession so that the ball carrier was hit as he was struggling to his feet. The drills were effective: one spring after three weeks, not one of the original forty-five participants was still on the team.[5]

3. Terry Orlick, *Winning Through Cooperation* (Washington D.C.: Acropolis, 1978), p. 31.
4. Emily Greenspan, *Little Winners: Inside the World of the Child Sports Star* (Boston: Little, Brown, 1983), p. 177.
5. Gary Shaw, *Meat on the Hoof: The Hidden World of Texas Football* (New York: St. Martin, 1972), p. 123.

The coaches also employed other methods to humble players into forfeiting their scholarships. The injured players, except those on the first teams, were forced to wear jerseys imprinted with red crosses. They were required to jog around the practice field during the complete workout. The coaches then complained about the guys who "couldn't take it," implying that their injuries were fake. But those on the first teams never wore the special jerseys and were never accused of imaginary ailments.

But the wounds from making "winners" are often more subtle. James Michener met a college-bound athlete who did not know the multiplication table, had never read a book, had no concept of history, and had no understanding of science. An overemphasis on winning abuses the "worthy" and the "unworthy" alike.

EROSION OF MORALS

Second, devotion to winning erodes the participants' morals. Former NBA star Willis Reed, upon resigning as head coach at Creighton University, discussed the cost of coaching a winner: "If you're going to stay in college basketball and be successful, you'll have to do some things I can't do."[6] Statistics support Reed's view—since 1952 more than half of NCAA Division 1 schools have been caught cheating.

Try to think of a famous coach who doesn't win consistently. Or try to think of a winning coach who is unknown. It's difficult. Someone once said that winning "covers a multitude of sins and not winning is simply un-

6. "Reed Resigns as Head Coach at Creighton," *Minneapolis Tribune*, 2 May 1985.

forgivable."[7] Winners are perceived as good guys simply because they win—though they may have acted despicably to succeed. When only the end result matters, the means will be judged pragmatically, not morally.

Does it matter if I lie about my child's age so that he can be successful among a younger group of athletes? Does it matter if I promise a young black man a good education but counsel him to take easy, meaningless courses to ensure his eligibility? Does it matter if I, as a coach, bend the rules so that my sons can have a winning team? Where will it end? A coach angered by the behavior of a fellow coach showed where such thinking leads:

> We have this must-play rule where every player is supposed to play a series every quarter. . . . This guy worked out a scheme whereby he'd send the poor player, No. 50, say, in with, say No. 60. The woman who checks the subs—we call her the watchdog—checks off 50 and 60, coming in. Then as soon as 50 gets to the huddle he turns around and runs back off with the player 60 was sent in for. The watchdog wasn't asked to check who went out, only who went in. No. 50 never played.[8]

The process *does* matter. It matters to No. 50 and to the other players who witness such deception. They are being given a number one grade lesson in the School of Winning—a school with a limited curriculum.

Christians in sports have also demonstrated expedience. We have used the witness of big-name athletes without knowing the depth of their commitment. We justify it by saying it will attract more children. But what

---

7. Charles Leerhsen, "Blitzing the Coaches," *Newsweek* 104, no. 22 (19 Nov. 1984): 66.
8. John Underwood, "Taking the Fun Out of a Game," in *Joy and Sadness in Children's Sports* (Champaign, Ill.: Human Kinetics, 1978), p. 60.

happens when that athlete promotes a brand of beer? Or is seen cursing a referee? Or later confesses that his interest in religion was just a fad? What happens in the hearts of the kids who heard his witness? The means (i.e., the processes) *do* matter.

DAMAGE TO SELF-ESTEEM

While watching a baseball tournament for preteen boys, I witnessed a game in which one of the teams was far superior. If I had been the coach of the weaker team I would have asked to see birth certificates! The weaker team's third baseman had to endure the brunt of the size difference as the bigger boys were able to pull the pitches in his direction. Third base was literally a "hot box," and the frustrated boy made several errors. In the middle of an especially bad inning, the coach got so exasperated that he removed the boy. The dejected boy dragged his feet into the dugout and buried his face in his glove. At the same time, the coach warned his replacement, "Now, don't *you* let me down!"

A third consequence of an overemphasis on winning is that it damages kids' self-esteem. Even though not every child can be a winner, we have made winning the only way to salvage self-esteem. Had that baseball coach been more sensitive, he could have encouraged his young player: "Hey, Johnny, I know you're doing your best. Our problem is that the New York Yankees were directed to the wrong stadium!"

Research has shown why losing is so devastating—we unconsciously view winners as good people and losers as bad people. Subjects viewed boxing matches, rating boxers according to maturity, appearance, worth, and potency. The winners were consistently rated higher than the losers.[9] Imagine what losing does to the self-esteem of kids when it is communicated to them that if they just had more character—not more skill—they would be winners, too.

ENCOURAGES NON-PARTICIPATION

Dropouts are a problem not only in school but also in sports. More than 75 percent of children have deserted formal sports by age fifteen.[10] Unfortunately, nonparticipation often extends into adulthood.

What causes this dropout rate? An emphasis on winning seems to be a main culprit. If winning is primary, kids who can't win won't compete. My middle son competes against his older brother in only those games that he perceives he has a chance to win.

Since success in sports is so highly valued, how do the "losers" manage? Many adjust by becoming fans. Terry Orlick said, "The winner-loser syndrome has paralyzed the average American into passive spectatordom. . . . The stakes are too high for most men to afford. It's safer for men to appoint surrogates to win for them while they watch the contest over a glass of beer."[11]

OVERLOOKS INDIVIDUAL PERFORMANCE

I attended Southern Methodist University in the late 1960s. During that period, the team normally lost as many games as it won. But what the team lacked in wins was compensated in excitement. One year, seven of their ten games were decided in the last two minutes of play. But in spite of such pulsating entertainment, tickets were

---

9. Thomas Tutko and William Bruns, *Winning Is Everything and Other American Myths* (New York: Macmillan, 1976), p. 8.
10. Orlick, p. 129.
11. Ibid., p. 131.

always plentiful. If the Mustangs had been able to beat Texas consistently, the stadium would have been jammed.

If fans pay attention only to winners, they will have to endure many boring games and will miss some of the more thrilling ones. That can be attested to in baseball as well: "No .400 hitter ever played on a pennant winner; of the 50 no-hit games thrown in American and National leagues during the first thirty years of the twentieth century, second division teams appeared in 49 of them; of seven unassisted triple plays, only one was made by a member of a pennant-winning club."[12]

The Olympic games have showcased the individual. But a growing emphasis on which countries win medals has obscured this. The Miller Brewing Company's slogan for 1984, Let's Win the Games Again, was an unfortunate position. If widely adopted, we will be unable to appreciate the performance of a foreigner such as Nadia Comaneci.

REMOVES FUN

My oldest son played on a championship soccer team. As the season progressed, the coaches scheduled extra practices and issued stern warnings about the next opponent. The parents attended the games with increasing consistency and enthusiasm, and the kids became more serious and determined. At the championship game, the intensity boiled over as the parents of the opposing teams exchanged heated words. What had happened? Somehow a shift had taken place—becoming champions had taken prominence over having fun.

The fun has been leached out of sports for many of

---

12. Bert R. Sugar, *Hit the Sign and Win a Free Suit of Clothes from Henry Finklestein* (New York: Macmillan, 1979), p. 43.

our performance-oriented Olympic athletes. It is reported that about 40 percent seek psychological help to handle the pressures of competition.[13] But the lack of fun is not limited to Olympic-caliber athletes. Most men are unable to enjoy the process of learning a sport.

> In tennis, for example, men are impatient to play matches, frequently shortchanging themselves on the practice rallies needed to develop consistency and form. In skiing, male beginners and intermediates are often found on slopes much too hard for them, helplessly and sometimes dangerously out of control; learning nothing at all; and except for the thrill of being afraid, not really enjoying themselves.[14]

OVERCONTROL BY ADULTS

Michael J. Ellis said, "Play has changed. . . . [It] has become more and more heavily managed and directed."[15]

Adult participation in youth sports can vastly improve a child's experience. But not all involvement is good. Adults have increasingly dominated children's sports by determining leagues, teams, rules, practices, and schedules. Such domination causes problems.

HINDERS SOCIALIZATION

Adult domination of children's play can retard their social skills. My wife and I recently recognized that our sons were too frequently asking us to judge their squab-

13. Greenspan, p. 195.
14. Mark Fasteau, "Sports: The Training Ground," in *Jock: Sports and Male Identity*, ed. Donald F. Sabo and Russ Runfola (Englewood Cliffs, N.J.: Prentice-Hall, 1980), p. 45.
15. Michael J. Ellis, *Why People Play* (Englewood Cliffs, N.J.: Prentice-Hall, 1973), p. 62.

bles. On one occasion our two older sons were playing with their blocks in the basement. I could hear their conversation heating up, and finally they came upstairs with a series of "I had it first" and "No you didn't." I calmly told them that they would have to work it out themselves and sent them back downstairs. The argument quickly resumed, as did the pleading for intervention. I repeated that it was their responsibility to solve it, and if they were unable to, the blocks would be put away. They groaned and complained but went back to trying to resolve the conflict. A few minutes later, I noticed that it was quiet in the basement. I went down and asked them how they worked it out. They explained that they did some digging in the box of blocks and discovered a similar block that one of them could use.

Opportunities to unravel conflicts may be denied on the playing field. Let's replay the backyard football game from chapter 1—but this time insert a typical adult. The first problem encountered by the kids was the selection of teams. The second graders complained that they were coerced into playing the third graders the week before. They refused to play again unless fair teams were chosen. But if an adult had been there the previous week, he would not have allowed such an unfair selection of teams. In fact, he might have chosen the teams himself. Remove lesson one on the need to organize the game fairly. Next, the children faced the dilemma of whether to play tackle or touch. The adult, noting the difference in size and the presence of girls, insists on touch. Remove a second lesson involving sensitivity. When controversies arise—"I touched you!"; "No you didn't!"—the adult acts as the sole arbiter. Remove a third lesson. Children will have difficulty learning to negotiate, to compromise, to judge, and to be sensitive unless they are given the freedom to do so.

LOSS OF CHILDHOOD

To become a world-class athlete, a child must begin training early. Parents usually become their managers, prodding them to give the necessary sacrifices. Assuming that a child could actually achieve, say, an Olympic medal, is that a suitable substitute for important childhood experiences? I think not.

All adult involvement in youth sports is not bad. Adults can help by offering encouragement and preventing injuries, such as warning children not to stand too close to a batter. They can model sports skills and godly attitudes. Children can greatly benefit from the *appropriate* involvement of adults.

CONCLUSION

Children's sports do not have to be dominated by a winning ethic or by adults. Those weaknesses *can* be changed.

3

Sports' Inherent Weaknesses

As a golfer I encounter a host of problems when I venture onto a course. Some of those could be overcome. My bad golf habits could be altered through practice (which I hate). A lack of distance in my drive could possibly be resolved by buying a new driver (though I doubt it). I could prevent slipping by purchasing a new pair of golf shoes (but I am too cheap). And I could develop a more positive attitude (but I enjoy complaining).

On the other hand, problems confront me that can't be changed. I can't fill in the sand trap where I invariably land. I can't chop down the tree that blocks my drive. I can't perform a Moses-like feat and dry up the river that swallows my golf ball. I can only adjust to such hazards.

The problems in sports are similar. Some can be changed (e.g., an overemphasis on winning), and others can't be changed without severely altering the structure of games. Such alteration is not necessary or realistic. Competitive games are inseparable from much of family, school, and community life. We must learn how to adapt to their influence.

THE PROBLEM OF COMPARISONS

My sons and I enjoy video games. But when we began playing years ago, it was a frustrating experience for them as they compared their skills to mine. (If comparisons were being made today, I would be the frustrated one!)

Sports repeatedly expose children to such comparisons, and those comparisons are often negative. In every game there will be at least one loser—and often many more. The percentage of losers continually increases as we play championships at the conference, regional, sectional, and national levels.

In the parable of the talents Jesus made clear that people have been given a unique combination of skills. But when children compare their performance with others, they don't usually take into account such differences.

A partial solution to the problem of comparisons is to measure a child's performance against his past performances. I used this concept to help my sons enjoy playing video games with me. When they didn't compare their scores with mine they were less frustrated. Encouraging a child to measure his performance by his past performances can also be done in other areas—the time he runs a race, the number of jumps he makes in a rope-jumping time trial, the number of times he kicks a ball in a soccer game, or the number of rebounds he makes in a basketball game.

Comparisons can be especially damaging to the recurrent loser. Tara Scanlan explains: "The important point is that many children engage in intense competition over extended periods of time with similar consequences being repeated over and over again. It is this repetition that makes developmental considerations relevant."[1] Childhood is a time in which to develop the sense of being able to do a job well. Repeated failure in sports may contribute to feelings of incompetence and unworthiness in children.

Yet you may ask, But isn't sports just one area of a child's life? Can't losers in sports raise their confidence in other activities? Some do—but many do not. The problem is that few other activities are so observable to parents and peers. Novelist James Michener, even though he was making A's in school, noted: "I cannot recall a single instance in which any member of my community gave me any accolades for such accomplishment. In Doylestown, in those days, all that mattered was sports, and even today across America things are not much different."[2] Such selective praise lessens the impact of achievement in nonsports activities.

The stress given to comparative differences will often determine how children are affected. Children—both losers *and* winners—can be ravaged by rewards for ability:

> Unless you give everyone the same kind of trophy, you're telling the loser, "You're different from the winner." But children know who the better ball players are. . . . To give out trophies simply accentuates this difference. It makes the youngster who doesn't have talent feel even less capable, and it gives a distorted perspective to the child who gets the higher trophy.[3]

The constant comparisons in sports must be carefully monitored. They can do great damage to children.

1. Tara Scanlan, "Social Evaluation: A Key Developmental Element in the Competition Process," in *Children in Sport*, ed. Richard Magill, Michael Ash, and Frank Smoll (Champaign, Ill.: Human Kinetics, 1982), p. 138.
2. James Michener, *Sports in America* (New York: Random, 1976), p. 6.
3. Thomas Tutko and William Bruns, *Winning Is Everything and Other American Myths* (New York: Macmillan, 1976), p. 63.

COMPENSATION

Rewards may influence a child's reason for participating in sports, as this incident shows.

> [An] old man lived alone on a street where boys played
> noisily every afternoon. One day the din became too
> much, and he called the boys into his house. He told
> them he liked to listen to them play, but his hearing
> was failing and he could no longer hear their games. He
> asked them to come around each day and play noisily
> in front of his house. If they did, he would give them
> each a quarter. The youngsters raced back the follow-
> ing day and made a tremendous racket in front of the
> house. The old man paid them, and asked them to re-
> turn the next day. Again they made noise, and again
> the old man paid them for it. But this time he gave
> each boy only 20 cents, explaining that he was running
> out of money. On the following day, they got only 15
> cents each. Furthermore, the old man told them, he
> would have to reduce the fee to five cents on the 4th
> day. The boys became angry, and told the old man they
> would not be back. It was not worth the effort, they
> said, to make noise for only five cents a day.[4]

Educational psychologists call this a shift from intrinsic
to extrinsic motivation. A child enters school enjoying the
process of learning. But when that learning is rewarded
with grades, he is now energized by the payoff. A child
may begin playing baseball because he loves the game
but have his attention grabbed by a potential trophy.

The issue of what motivates a child to take part in
sports is important because only a handful of children
will receive all-state honors or media coverage—and even

---

4. Rainer Martens, "Kids Sports: A Den of Iniquity or Land of Promise," in
   Magill, Ash, and Smoll, p. 209.

those rewards pass quickly. NBC cameras will probably not cover basketball games played by middle-aged men at the local YMCA. If a person's participation in sports is based on external rewards, he may quit playing when those rewards are not available.

COMPETITIVENESS

Is competitiveness a problem? Former president Gerald Ford doesn't think so. He said that the competitive spirit has "made us great." As a result, he believes that "there are few things more important to a country's growth and well-being than competitive athletics."[5]

A strong competitive drive—especially among men —has been traditionally viewed as an asset. That belief accounts for the fact that "competition pervades almost all aspects of American society. The work world, sports, courtship, organizations like the Cub Scouts, and schools all thrive on competition."[6]

When parents extol competitiveness, they usually do so thinking that it will provide their child with the motivation to strive after life's limited rewards. Not everyone can be a millionaire. Not everyone can be a mayor. Not everyone marries the homecoming king or queen. Not everyone can make it to college. Many hope that competitive sports will teach children skills that will be instrumental in claiming such prizes.

Jesus made clear that life is a challenge. He told His disciples, "Enter through the narrow gate. For wide is the gate and broad is the road that leads to destruction, and many enter through it. But small is the gate and narrow

---

5. Wilbert M. Leonard II, *A Sociological Perspective of Sport* (Minneapolis: Burgess, 1980), p. 70.
6. D. Stanley Eitzen and George H. Sage, *The Sociology of American Sport* (Dubuque, Iowa: William C. Brown, 1978), p. 62.

the road that leads to life, and only a few find it" (Matthew 7:13-14). The question then is not whether children need the motivation to tackle life's difficult tasks but whether sports produce an enthusiasm for such work.

COMPETITION AND LIFE'S CHALLENGES

It is believed that competition produces children who are eager for a challenge. But is that *consistently* true? As we have seen, repeated failure normally causes kids to avoid a challenge. Fear of failure can prevent children from trying: "In the gymnasium they may refuse to participate, become ill, complain of injury, or hide in line to avoid their turn. When pressured into making an attempt, they respond with a half-hearted effort that shows the others they aren't trying, for it's not so bad to fail if you don't really try."[7]

One sports psychologist asked, "Have we not . . . directed our sole attention to the winners and ignored the effects of competition upon losers who, as we have seen, constitute at least half the participants?"[8] It may be that the extolling of competition has come from the winners.

Furthermore, even though competition may encourage the pursuit of excellence in some children, it is not the only way, or possibly, the best way. In one representative study, students were asked to perform the same task in either a competitive or a cooperative group. The children in the cooperative group were more helpful and friendly with each other, which resulted in a more favorable view of the group and a greater feeling of being liked.

7. Hollis Fait and John Billing, "Reassessment of the Value of Competition," in *Joy and Sadness in Children's Sport*, ed. Rainer Martens (Champaign, Ill.: Human Kinetics, 1978), p. 101.
8. Ibid., p. 100.

The group also turned out a superior product, which more of the kids felt they had had a hand in.[9]

Excellence can be achieved in a cooperative environment.

THE DARK SIDE OF COMPETITIVENESS

But even if sports establish an enthusiasm for life's challenges, there would still be concern, because competition may also generate self-orientation and hostility.

Self-orientation. Studies have concluded that competition nurtures "me-ism." The point is not that everyone who competes is self-centered, but that competition incorporates a tendency toward self-concern. If you and I are striving for the same prize, I don't expect you to act generously in my behalf. In fact, if you become sympathetic while winning, you may ease up, allowing me to overtake you. If so, you will be chided for lacking a "killer's instinct."

But don't team sports counteract self-orientation? Yes and no. Team sports offer greater—but not exclusive—opportunities for cooperation. A former college football player divulged his joy in learning that a teammate was having scholastic problems: "I even remember figuring out on paper who my competition would be the next year and what their chances were of making it scholastically. I remember how elated I was my third year when I found out a guy I was battling for second team had left school because of bad grades."[10]

9. Terry Orlick, *Winning Through Cooperation* (Washington, D.C.: Acropolis, 1978), p. 31.
10. Gary Shaw, *Meat on the Hoof: The Hidden World of Texas Football* (New York: St. Martin, 1972), p. 60.

Within a team there is rivalry to be the leading scorer, to gain playing time, to receive recognition. It is difficult to be wholly concerned about the welfare of teammates when their success may contribute to your failure.

One well-known gymnastic coach explained his philosophy of instruction: "Pressure is everything. We teach the girls that they can't slow down in training for even a day, because their roommate or somebody else will eat them up alive in competition. They've got to be careful, or their best friend will beat them."[11]

Like the immovable sand trap, a bent toward self-seeking cannot be eradicated from sports. But the way parents, coaches, and children adjust to the "trap" will determine the extent to which the individual is influenced.

Hostility. If my concern is for my own success and you are a threat to that, I may develop ill feelings toward you. Research has confirmed that unfriendly acts between participants increase during competition. Only 11 percent of a group of boys' interactions were unfriendly in their natural environment. But in a competitive game, unfriendly acts ballooned to 42 percent.[12]

The greatest hostility is reserved for those who most often thwart our goals. There is little love exchanged between the Dallas Cowboys and the Washington Redskins. Why? Because both have frustrated the other numerous times in attempting to win championships. I have heard little about the Redskins hating the Seattle Seahawks. The Seahawks haven't been a major nemesis of the Redskins.

11. Bob Abel and Mike Valenti, *Sports Quotes: The Inside View of the Sports World* (New York: Facts on File, 1983), p. 46.
12. Donna Gelfand and Donald Hartmann, "Some Detrimental Effects of Competitive Sports on Children's Behavior," in Magill, Ash, and Smoll, p. 198.

Some have theorized that sports act as a release for aggression. The view is that by allowing aggression as an outlet on the playing field, society will be spared more destructive means (e.g., war) of venting hostility. The president of the National Hockey League apparently believes that theory: "The spontaneous fight that breaks out as a result of frustration is an outlet. To eliminate that outlet is to bring about retaliation in more severe form."[13] What is he thinking—that players will wait outside the arena to blow away opponents with a bazooka?

Research indicates that sports are frequently a stimulant to, rather than a repressor of, aggressive feelings. Even watching some sporting events can increase a person's aggression.

Unfortunately, the hostility aroused within competition may be transferred to non-game settings. Sherif's study on the effects of prolonged competition at a summer camp confirmed that hostility aroused during competition can be carried beyond the playing field: "Raids and acts of aggression were organized by the boys themselves. Such acts included messing up the rival's cabin, painting derogatory slogans on the stolen blue jeans of the opponent's leader and hoarding small green apples to be used 'in case' of attack." When one team was declared the overall winner, "boys in each group possessed attitudes of extreme prejudice and hostility, universally condemning the individual characters of members of their rival group."[14]

Not all competition produces high levels of hostility, but the potential is there.

13. Abel and Valenti, p. 24.
14. Carolyn Sherif, "The Social Context of Competition," in Martens, p. 92.

Competitiveness and assertive behavior. This critique of competitiveness does not conclude that we should teach our children to have a tread-on-me attitude. Though Jesus was willing to turn the other cheek, He could also brandish a whip.

Assertiveness can be nurtured. Recently our ten-year-old son wanted to surprise us by making lunch. He concocted a dish called "baked bean soup." I never had the courage to ask what he put into it. The way we respond to our kids' creative initiatives—whether it is baking a cake, writing a poem, or styling their own hair—will determine whether they are able to assert themselves and their ideas. If we want our children to be enthused about life's challenges, we will have to think creatively about how to encourage such confidence.

Competitiveness and cooperativeness. A husband talked about the tension in his dying marriage:

> I didn't really know that Susan and I were in competition. We never fought but we continually struggled: who would do the shopping? Who the cleaning? Who would sleep late? Who would nap? Who would take care of the children? . . . If Susan was victorious—got a nap, say—I would begrudge her success. If I succeeded, Susan would be resentful. . . . As the struggle wore on I wore out and began to look for intimacy elsewhere. Eventually the competition ended. This time everybody lost.[15]

It is unfortunate that we have not stressed cooperativeness in our culture. The ability to serve others forms

---

15. R. C. Townsend, "The Competitive Male as Loser," in *Jock: Sports and Male Identity,* ed. Donald F. Sabo and Russ Runfola (Englewood Cliffs, N.J.: Prentice-Hall, 1980), p. 278.

the basis of New Testament Christianity. We are admonished to love, encourage, support, help, submit, and pray for one another. That mutual support is not *naturally* encouraged in competitive games. It will take concentrated effort by parents to help their children build cooperative skills—whether in sports or out of sports.

CONCLUSION

The weaknesses of competitive sports do not demand its elimination. When it is said that competitive sports bend participants toward self-interest, it doesn't mean that we must throw up our hands, forever surrendering our children to the clutches of selfishness. When it is said that sports produce comparisons that are dangerous to the "losers," it doesn't mean that sports should be abandoned to the skilled. It simply means that sports' faults must be recognized and countered in meaningful ways. The following chapters will discuss how that can be done.

Part 2

The Parent's Role

4

Organizing Children's Sports

Jack Kramer, the former tennis star, remembers the influence of his father:

> One time when I was just starting to win, I began to think I was a big shot, and I carried on a running argument with the umpire. When he called me for a foot fault, I blew my stack altogether and threw my racket over the fence. I looked up then and saw my father approaching the umpire's chair. I felt like a million dollars: my old man was going to show this guy that his boy couldn't be pushed around. Yes sir!
>
> After a few seconds of conferring with Dad, the referee suddenly stood up, waved his arms, and announced that the match was over, the win going to my opponent by default. My father had called it off. Our discussion was brief. "Son," he said, "you ever do that again, you'll never go back on a tennis court as long as you live in my house."[1]

1. Jack Kramer, *The Game* (New York: G. P. Putnam, 1979), p. 23.

Parent, you can have a powerful influence on your child's participation in sports. To a large extent, you will determine whether he is most affected by sports' strengths or weaknesses. It all begins by organizing sports properly.

ORGANIZING SPORTS

Soccer is prospering in our city. Registrations increase yearly. There are willing coaches. Parents turn out in droves to watch their kids play. The city generously maintains excellent facilities. But in spite of such popularity, our teams haven't always done well at state tournaments. While watching a recent state tournament, my wife talked with a spectator from the city that wins most of the championships. The spectator explained that soccer registrations were way down in her city. They were producing champions but apparently at the expense of general interest in the sport.

The way youth sports are organized will often determine whether kids have good experiences or not. It is the organization that controls the emphasis given to winning. It is the organization that decides how kids will be rewarded. It is the organization that conducts banquets. It is the organization that trains referees and establishes the league rules. Not everyone can influence such foundational principles. But becoming involved in your league's structure may reap great benefits for your child.

DE-EMPHASIZE WINNING

Your daughter comes to bat in the last inning with her team behind by a run. The bases are loaded, and there are two outs. She strikes out. Will she be crushed by her failure? The answer, in part, is determined by the importance of that game. Research has concluded that competing is fun when winning isn't a life-or-death matter. A girl can handle the stress of coming to bat at the crux of a game *if* the game is not being played for the championship of the Milky Way! Researchers observed professional football games to record instances of helping behavior between opponents. Throughout the regular season, games assistance (e.g., one player helping an opposing player off the ground) was frequently given. But during the Super Bowl that year, there was not a single incident of helping.[2] The structure of the game hadn't changed—only its meaning.

When I know that my sons will be playing in championship games, I try to avoid talking a lot about it in the preceding days. Because the more the outcome is stressed, the more it will stress the participants.

An emphasis on winning can be lessened through legislation that elevates people over winning. For example, every youth league should have a rule that suspends anyone who verbally or physically abuses an official. That includes coaches, players, and *especially* parents.

Another rule placing the priority on people is one that gives equal playing time to all children. Ninety percent of a group of children indicated that they would rather play on a losing team than sit on the bench of a winning team.[3] Kids want to play. And youth sports should be organized to let them play.

It is ironic that even if youth sports programs were designed to develop Olympic champions, a policy of playing the best would not be wisest. A twelve-year study revealed that only one in four children who were stars as

2. B. Berg, "Helping Behavior on the Gridiron: It Helps If You're Winning," *Psychology Reports* 42 (1978): 531.
3. Ronald E. Smith and Frank L. Smoll, *Kidsports: A Survival Guide for Parents* (Reading, Mass.: Addison-Wesley, 1983), p. 11.

children were also stars in adolescence.[4] Often that discrepancy can be traced to different rates of maturity.

Sitting on the bench can have devastating consequences for a child. First, he may feel inferior, believing that "if he were more talented, he would be on the first string. He must face this embarrassment not only with his peers, who are clearly aware of it, but with his parents as well."[5]

Also, when the child is barred from playing, his skills are stunted. Thus, the gap between kids spreads, convincing the substitute of his inferiority. Our priorities are wrong. James Michener said, "We place an undue emphasis on gifted athletes aged 15 to 22, a preposterous emphasis on a few professionals aged 23 to 35, and never enough on the mass of our population."[6] We can begin to place the emphasis on the wider population by giving children equal playing time.

But regulations alone won't ensure a de-emphasis on winning. Some coaches have evaded rules of equal play by asking certain kids to stay home from an important game. Or the coaches and the stronger players have begrudged the weaker players' right to play—"Oh, no! Smith hasn't played yet? Are we in trouble now!" A Pharisaical commitment to the letter but not the spirit of the law will be as destructive as an absence of good rules.

A coach can go beyond the requirements by letting children play a variety of positions. After all, no child will want to play right field or lineman all the time. One football coach explained his reasoning: "Running the ball, throwing it, catching a pass, making touchdowns—those

---

4. Emily Greenspan, *Little Winners: Inside the World of the Child Sports Star* (Boston: Little, Brown, 1983), p. 167.
5. Thomas Tutko and William Bruns, *Winning Is Everything and Other American Myths* (New York: Macmillan, 1976), p. 85.
6. James Michener, *Sports in America* (New York: Random, 1976), p. 17.

are the things kids think of as football."[7]

Playing multiple positions is not only fun but also agrees with kids' long-range development. Many who are too slow, too small, or too uncoordinated to play a certain position will not be so when their bodies mature. But without prior experience they will have little chance of success.

But care must be taken. While coaching soccer, I let an untested boy play goalie. The other team quickly scored three goals, and he was so distraught he almost quit the team.

MINIMIZE ORGANIZATION

When my older sons began to play football together, the games ended quickly because the elder was consistently beating the younger—who opted for non-participation rather than failure. When the older one complained about his brother's refusals to play, I explained that he would have to adjust the rules to entice his brother to play. A few days later, the two of them came bursting in the back door with a football. The older one proclaimed that his younger brother had beaten him at a game of football. Amazed, I asked how it happened. The younger one, smiling, explained: "Well, he had to tackle me. I only had to touch him." That night I was able to tell my eldest how proud I was—and Jesus was—of his efforts to make the game fun for his brother. A child's ability to relate sensitively to others can be enhanced by such minimally organized sports.

Organized sports may not give kids an opportunity to develop the basic skills of their sport. Adults may put a

7. John Underwood, "Taking the Fun Out of a Game," in *Joy and Sadness in Children's Sports,* ed. Rainer Martens (Champaign, Ill.: Human Kinetics, 1978), p. 62.

child "in a situation where he must learn to perform skills under pressure before he is comfortable with the sport. . . . The child who just wants to learn how to pick up a ground ball and throw it correctly to first base is confounded by the fact that he has to throw out the runner and kill a rally."[8]

Hall of Fame pitcher Robin Roberts believes that baseball at the Little League age should be "a softball thrown overhand where a boy can hit fifteen times a game, with no walks and strike-outs. They should be running and sliding into bases. The score should be 42-38."[9]

Unfortunately, it may be easier to point the finger at the structure of youth sports than to offer solutions. It is unrealistic to think that organized sports will suddenly disappear. The best solution may be to offer less organized alternatives.

A minimally organized sports event occurred at my oldest son's soccer team picnic when the parents challenged the kids to a game of soccer. The game lasted over two hours and would have gone on longer if it had been a lighted field. The only regrets registered were by the out-of-shape parents the next morning!

My three sons dragged me into another low-structured sports experience one sizzling, summer day. I had spent the morning clipping our shaggy lawn and was covered with bits of itchy grass, a layer of dust, and rivers of sweat. My sons easily hastened me to an afternoon of swimming. But my vision of snoozing by the pool—interrupted only by an occasional cooling dunk—was not shared by them. They coaxed me into playing a game of "keep away" with their friends. I'm glad that their persuasion and my parental guilt got me off my lounge chair.

8. Greenspan, p. 38.
9. Michener, p. 107.

Though the age span approached forty years, it didn't keep any of us from having a grand time. We raced after stray throws. We leaped out of the water to try to block an opponent's toss. We delighted in seeing the smaller ones miraculously steal the ball from the bigger ones. My four year old, who didn't even know how to swim, was joyously bobbing in the midst of all that activity with an inner tube around his middle. That swimming pool was filled with more laughter than water. How could we have had more fun? By establishing a league and finding coaches and conducting practices and writing a rule book and keeping standings and—how ridiculous! But it isn't far from what we have done to many children's games.

As further alternatives, children can be encouraged to arrange neighborhood games after school or on weekends. Or set up a parent-child softball game for Saturday mornings. The alternatives are endless. But a child's time is limited. It may be necessary to limit his organized sports to give time for the less organized variety.

EQUALIZE TEAMS

A third principle of organization is to make the teams as equal as possible. A while back I played in a two-day team golf tournament. Our team of four golfers included a novice. By the time we were on the third tee we knew that he could not help the team at all—even if we had doubled his handicap! Since the team's performance relied on each person's contribution, we all became discouraged.

Research has found that competing is fun when kids feel they have a reasonable chance of winning.[10] Watch

10. David Johnson and Roger Johnson, "Cooperative, Competitive, and Individualistic Learning," *Journal of Research and Development* 12, no. 1 (1978): 11.

what happens when a team is a recurrent loser. The kids' movements are labored. They begin to bicker among themselves. The coach may have difficulty getting them to the games. To counter inequality, some leagues have developed a rating system of the players. One coach explained the impact of such an approach on his league: "Something happened. . . . We got along great the whole year. The league was tight, and I think we all had fun. I know my kids did. You'd see 'em during a game running back to the huddle and sliding in on their pads. It didn't look like the Dolphins, but it was fun."[11]

Equality within teams is nearly as important as equality between teams. Though the primary competition takes place between teams, there is also jockeying within the team for playing time or certain positions. Within a team, equality can be achieved by grouping kids in narrow age groups (e.g., nine and ten year olds rather than nine through twelve year olds), according to their height and weight, or according to their skill level. Our soccer association has begun an advanced league that allows the less skilled kids to develop their abilities in a recreational league.

A philosophy of in-team equality should encourage boys and girls to have separate leagues. Even though pre-teen girls are equal to boys in their natural abilities, boys —who are rewarded more for sports success—have frequently done more with that ability.

MINIMIZE EXTERNAL REWARDS

When rewards are accentuated, children's attention may be drawn to the payoff rather than to the games themselves.

11. John Underwood, "Taking the Fun Out of a Game," in Martens, p. 63.

A picture comes to mind of a country fair at which children were searching through a haystack in which small gifts had been randomly distributed. If a child found a gift, he could keep it, but had to leave. Many a child did just that. They searched, found their reward, and left happily smiling. But there were some others, although few, who searched, found a gift, quickly hid it again in the straw, and continued searching. For them, searching was the reward![12]

The fourth principle of organization is to minimize external rewards (e.g., trophies and all-star teams) so that kids aren't stripped of the joy of playing. Stressing rewards reinforces the differences between children. That can be particularly damaging to the unathletic child.

The first year that our oldest son played basketball, the league had a city tournament. His team lost their first game but received ribbons for participation. Olympic champions could not have been more pleased! Six years later my son still displays that ribbon on his bulletin board. If rewards are given, let them be for participation and effort rather than for winning or skill.

DEVELOP CREATIVE STRUCTURES

Many believe that tampering with the structure of a game is tantamount to challenging the Ten Commandments. But there should be freedom to adjust the games to meet children's needs. Watch grade school children strain to shoot a basket on a ten-foot hoop. But why does the basket have to be ten feet high? We have a basket in our backyard that is about eight feet above the ground. My sons have played since they were five. It has been bet-

12. Joseph Levy, *Play Behavior* (New York: John Wiley, 1978), p. 7.

ter for their form, skill development, and especially for their ego. (And it allows Dad to feel like the six-foot, ten-inch player he longed to be when he was growing up!)

A fifth organizational principle is to develop creative structures that enhance youth sports. In Canada, where hockey is overwhelmingly the national sport, some youth hockey programs don't allow the scores or individual records to be kept. In a Midwestern town, the following rule changes were made in a youth softball league. The percentage of parents who were either supportive of or neutral toward the change is indicated.[13]

No strikeouts	74%
Use a softer ball	79%
Mandatory player rotation	96%
No score kept	60%
No win-loss records	78%

Some Little Leagues use a pitching machine. It cuts out the walks, thus giving batters and fielders more practice. It also limits the fear of being hit by a pitched ball.

Soccer purists shuddered when an indoor soccer league was formed. But the fast-paced and higher scoring game has been popular. The NFL adjusted its rules to place more emphasis on the forward pass. Baseball instituted the designated hitter to bat for the pitcher. Rules are not set in concrete. They should be changed if kids will benefit.

---

13. David Laurie and Charles Corbin, "Parental Attitudes Concerning Modifications in Baseball for Young Children," *The Physical Educator* (May 1981): 107.

5

Guiding Children's Selection of Sports

Bill Veeck, former owner of the Chicago White Sox, once said, "Baseball is the only game left for people. To play basketball now, you have to be seven-foot-six. To play football you have to be the same width."

Individual differences are important in selecting a sport. A good selection will enhance a child's experience —a bad one, the opposite. "Which sport is best for my child? At what age should he begin? How much should he participate?" The answers to those questions should help you guide your child's selection of a sport.

WHEN: CHILDREN'S READINESS FOR SPORTS

When I was a boy, I had no opportunity to participate in organized sports until I reached the age of nine. Today, children can begin at the age of five. Is that wise? When are children ready for organized competition?

THE NEED FOR SUCCESS

Jacob was a large, lumbering boy who was assigned to my fifth-grade basketball team. At the first practice his mother apologized twice for her boy's ineptness. As the season developed I noticed that her attitude had seeped into her son who meekly deflected all my compliments —"Oh, it wasn't such a good shot, just lucky." But Jacob was a hustler, and his size made him an adequate rebounder. As I selectively praised his abilities, the personal put-downs faded, and Jacob became a happy, enthusiastic participant. Time and again I have seen success build confidence in young children. Sports psychologist William Beausay believes that success is especially important for preteen children:

> Competitive sport has [no] place in the development of a child before age thirteen. All children need a series of happy, victorious experiences. The normal defeats will come in the routine give-and-take of their own play. But they must learn to succeed before they can accept defeat. After thirteen, they then must be defeated to instigate further growth.[1]

Now it may not be necessary or practical to keep a child out of organized sports until the teen years, but Beausay's main point—that kids need success—is what must be noted.

Success is important for young children because they can't reason effectively. When our middle son, Andrew, began to make friends, he had two demoralizing encounters. One time he was at a friend's house, and the boy ordered Andrew to go home because he wanted to play with someone else. A few days later, he went to play

1. Gary Warner, *Competition* (Elgin, Ill.: David C. Cook, 1979), p. 330.

with another boy, and the boy's older friend beat up Andrew. My wife and I found him hiding and crying in the back closet—too ashamed to face us. Words could not convince him that not all children are like that, or that those boys would not always treat him the same way. His confidence in making friends was revived only after we had engineered several successful experiences.

Similarly, if a young child fails in sports, it is hard for him to reason that he will be good at something else or some other sport, or that sport is not that important. Thus, in answering the question of when kids should begin competition, parents should remember that younger children are easily damaged by failure.

FAMILY NEEDS

Next week is tournament week for our sons' soccer teams. Potentially, we could attend ten games in six days. In thinking about when kids should begin organized sports, it is important to remember the cost to a family. It will change meal times, evening activities, and vacation schedules. Mom may have to apply for a chauffeur's license. A non-participating child may feel neglected. For some of those reasons, we decided to keep our sons out of competition until they were eight years old. As it is, we feel relieved when the seasons are over so that we have more family time.

ORGANIZED VERSUS UNORGANIZED

Delaying children's involvement in organized sports does not mean that they can't or shouldn't have opportunity to learn sports skills at early ages. Vermont ski coach Mickey Cochran, in discussing how he taught his own children to ski, explained that they needed a great deal of patience, "which took some real tongue-biting at times.

We would just about have their skis on and they would say, 'I have to go to the bathroom' or 'I want a drink of water.' " He and his wife wanted skiing to be fun for their kids. After all, Cochran reasoned, "it may be that they don't have a hankering to be Jean Claude Killy or a Henry Aaron."[2]

If kids have not learned how to throw and catch a ball before they go to school, they may be in trouble. One wise nursery school administrator advises parents to teach their kids sports skills before they get to school because unathletic children are often ridiculed by their classmates.

What: Choosing a Sport

Rugby underwent major rule changes in the nineteenth century. They included:[3]

Rule XIV. No hacking with the heel, unless below the knee.

Rule XV. No one wearing projecting nails or iron plates on the soles of or heels of his shoes or boots shall be allowed to play.

Rule XXII. A player standing up to another may hold one arm only, but he may hack him or knock the ball out of his hands if he attempts to kick it.

Imagine being a parent in nineteenth-century England with choices like that! Fortunately, there are presently a host of fun and safe sports for children.

2. Thomas Tutko and William Burns, *Winning Is Everything and Other American Myths* (New York: Macmillan, 1976), p. 57.
3. Don Atyeo, *Blood and Guts: Violence in Sports* (New York: Paddington, 1979), p. 198.

THINK ABOUT A LIFETIME

Leisure is important to us throughout our lives. Think about what sports you see people playing in their forties, fifties, sixties, and even higher. I think of tennis, golf, racquetball, swimming, cross-country skiing, running, and bicycling. I have yet to see a hockey league for senior citizens! Your child should be encouraged to learn at least one of those lifetime sports.

Once again, first experiences are crucial in determining a person's attitude toward a particular sport. A sport must be introduced carefully to ensure a long-term enjoyment of it.

THINK ABOUT EXERCISE

Medical experts report an alarming increase in heart problems among the young. Vigorous exercise through sports like track, soccer, ice skating, or basketball provides the strenuous exercise that is needed to deter heart disease. If a child is interested in a sport such as golf, he should also be encouraged to swim, bike, or walk. Parents, you don't need to be chauffeurs. If at all possible, let your child transport himself to school, ball practice, or a friend's house.

Because the benefits of exercise are short-lived—in a few weeks the strength and endurance built through exercise evaporate—my wife and I want to build a *habit* of exercise in our sons. Therefore, our routines include physical activity. Family time might include a game of kickball or Frisbee. Before dinner we might chase our cocker spaniel—whose idea of retrieving is to get a stick in his mouth and try to elude our grasp. Our vacations offer a heavy dose of exercise—climbing mountains, hiking, swimming, and skating.

THINK ABOUT PHYSICAL HEALTH

Can there be too much of a good thing? If jogging is good for a child, what about running in a marathon? What is the effect of strenuous exercise on the child's heart, lungs, muscles, and bones?

Children's hearts cause no concern—they are able to withstand any test of endurance. But other parts of the body are more vulnerable, especially joints that require repetitive action (e.g., the shoulders of baseball pitchers and swimmers and the knees of basketball players). The "cumulative wear and tear on the joints often leads to chronic injuries," which can result in "pain, tendonitis, and sometimes changes in bone structure that can last a lifetime."[4] Thus, the demands may become too great if those actions are repeated too often.

Furthermore, a sport must be evaluated by its injury potential. I want to encourage my sons to play sports in which serious injury seldom occurs. For that reason, I will not support a desire to play football or hockey. Comedian Rodney Dangerfield alluded to the rough nature of hockey when he quipped, "I went to a fight the other night and a hockey game broke out."[5] I am not on a crusade against those sports. But I see no reason to incline children toward a sport that commonly causes serious injuries.

Serious injury in football does not happen infrequently. Hayden Fry, the head coach of the University of Iowa football team, has said:

> From a human standpoint, I really question the game of football. It didn't used to be that bad. But with all

4. Emily Greenspan, *Little Winners: Inside the World of the Child Sports Star* (Boston: Little, Brown, 1983), p. 178.
5. Bob Abel and Mike Valenti, *Sports Quotes: The Inside View of the Sports World* (New York: Facts on File, 1983), p. 25.

the strength, technique, weight-lifting programs, and good diets that players have today, they have far surpassed their protective equipment.

It's really a physical game today. Your heart goes out to the players. I don't care who they are or where they play, sooner or later they're going to get wounded.[6]

The National Athletic Injury/Illness Reporting System (NAIRS) confirms Fry's statement. NAIRS reports that more than 10 percent of the participants suffer a major injury each year.[7] If that is multiplied by the number of years that a boy plays football, one can readily see the probability of a major injury occurring.

When our oldest son was two years old, he fell off a slide and received a concussion. We took the concussion seriously. After the doctor carefully examined him, he instructed us to watch for bleeding and to wake him every two hours the first night to make sure he wasn't going into a coma. The next few days were a tense time around our home. But concussions in football are treated as insignificant—"Oh, he just had his bell rung." NAIRS seldom reports concussions because they only minimally effect participation. But concussions are serious. Twenty career concussions with some strange side effects convinced Roger Staubach that it was time to quit professional football.

Many believe that football could be made safer. But apparently sports administrators remain committed to the status quo because they are afraid to tamper with a

6. "Iowa's Fry Appalled by Injuries," *Sioux Falls Argus Leader*, 12 Nov. 1984.
7. W. Buckley, "NAIRS: An Epidemiological Overview of the Severity of Injuries in College Football 1975-1980 Seasons," *Journal of Sports Behavior* 4 (1981): 157.

marketable product—which accounts for 75 percent of the funding for intercollegiate activities at major colleges.

Hockey has similar statistics on injuries. The Canadian Ophthalmological Society tested the eyesight of pro hockey players and found thirty-seven blind in one eye as a result of injuries.[8] Hockey, too, could be made much safer for the players by severely penalizing any type of violent behavior. But, again, the popularity of the game and fear of fan rejection may account for a reluctance to change.

THINK ABOUT MENTAL HEALTH

Though as a parent I am concerned about physical injury, I am more concerned about psychological injury. Sports' impact on this issue has been dealt with earlier —but there are two other yardsticks to use in measuring the influence of sports on the emotional life of your child.

Coaches. Research indicates that coaches have a varying impact on the mental health of children. It was found that:[9]

- baseball coaches were the least self-oriented and swimming and wrestling coaches were the most self-oriented
- baseball coaches were highest in affiliation orientation and gymnastics and football coaches were the lowest
- hockey and baseball coaches rated having fun significantly higher than swimming, wrestling, and gymnastics coaches

8. Abel and Valenti, p. 23.
9. Rainer Martens and Daniel Gould, "Why Do Adults Volunteer to Coach Children's Sports?" in *Psychology of Motor Behavior and Sport*, ed. Glyn C. Roberts and Karl M. Newell (Champaign, Ill.: Human Kinetics, 1979), pp. 85-87.

- baseball, basketball, soccer, and hockey coaches rated winning significantly lower than wrestling coaches

Those results are only suggestive of possible trends. The best advice is to check carefully on an individual coach or program to find out what emphasis is put on winning, having fun, and developing skills.

Stress on children. How does competitive stress affect the mental health of children? It depends on the amount. Moderate levels of stress usually enhance the experience (e.g., kids enjoy becoming excited), but high levels can be damaging to their emotional health—and to their performance. As expected, individual sports create more stress than team sports. Former Olympic skating champion Peggy Fleming talked about the pressure in her sport: "In four minutes of free skating you're being judged on a whole year of practice. Not many sports put you through that, being the focal point of the entire arena. You've got to look like you're enjoying yourself and accept the judges' decision and not throw a tomato at them. It's tough."[10]

A study of adolescent females competing in eight different sports found that gymnastics was the most stressful, followed by track and field, swimming, tennis, softball, volleyball, basketball, and field hockey.[11] Therefore, while a child is developing his self-confidence, it would be best to guide his organized participation toward team sports. He can begin learning the individual sports but should be kept out of most direct competition.

It might be thought that there would be less stress on good athletes, and, as a result, they would be able to han-

10. Abel and Valenti, p. 48.
11. M. R. Griffin, "An Analysis of State and Trait Anxiety Experienced in Sports Competition at Different Age Levels," *Foil* (Spring 1972): 61.

dle the increased anxiety found in individual sports. But studies have found no correlation between anxiety and a child's ability.[12] It is possible that the better athletes simply have more expected of them.

Because of the issue of stress, my wife and I have been pleased with our sons' involvement in soccer. Standing on a soccer field, a child can be watching the clouds fly by or trying to find a four-leaf clover, but few (other than the child's parents) notice. Kids are seldom put in the spotlight as they are when they come to bat in a baseball game or when they have to make a putt in golf.

THINK ABOUT YOUR CHILD'S ABILITY

If your sixth-grade daughter is already five feet eight inches tall, weighs 140 pounds, and is not coordinated, you wouldn't want to persuade her to take ballet lessons. Kids should select a sport that catches their interest *and* fits their abilities. Unfortunately, they normally choose a sport on the basis of parental or sibling models.

Our oldest son is aggressive, coordinated, and will probably grow quite tall. Basketball seems to be an ideal sport for his talents. Our middle son has the endurance of a South Dakota winter. Even his older brother—who like most older brothers has a hard time passing out compliments to a younger brother—marvels at his stamina on bike rides. Endurance sports such as track or bicycling seem to be made for him. The opportunities for their success are greater in a sport that fits their talents.

HOW MUCH: A CHILD'S TIME COMMITMENT TO SPORTS

A teenage Olympic champion swimmer had a weekday schedule in which she swam from 5:30 to 7:00 A.M.,

12. Tara Scanlan and Michael Passer, "Sources of Competitive Stress in Young Female Athletes," *Journal of Sport Psychology* 1 (1979): 157.

rushed to school, returned home at 1:30 P.M., caught a nap, ate dinner at 3:00, worked out again from 4:30 to 7:30, crawled home, had a snack, and fell into bed. On weekends she labored even longer in the pool. Is it good to let a child's sporting life become so dominant? I think not.

First, such dedication is unwise because the cost of making it to the top has ballooned—no longer can the gifted athlete ride on his natural abilities. He must "train hard year-round to meet the escalating standard. World records in track and field and swimming are broken almost as soon as they are established. The record-breaking time that won Mark Spitz a gold medal in the 100-meter freestyle at the 1972 Olympics wouldn't even qualify him for the event today."[13] Thus, even among those willing to make such sacrifices, few will reach their goals.

Furthermore, sole devotion to sports may be unwise. One study compared the SAT scores of two groups of high school athletes. One group's extracurricular activities were confined to sports. The other's included a diversity of activities. The SAT scores were lower for boys involved in sports only.[14] A child who narrowly strengthens sports skills may be weakened in other areas. Our kids need to exercise other skills. They must learn how to care for others. They need time to develop a walk with Christ. They need opportunities to explore the world of work. They need time to nurture their minds through study. When asking how much time our children should give to their sporting life, we must determine whether they have sufficient time for meeting the other tasks of childhood.

13. Greenspan, p. 27.
14. Daniel Landers, et al., "Socialization Via Interscholastic Athletics: Its Effects on Education," *Research Quarterly* 49 (1978): 480.

6

Guiding the Participation of Children

My wife observed a father helping his young son with his soccer skills. The father was kicking the ball to his son, who was instructed to trap the ball and kick it quickly back. The father bellowed a string of negative comments: "Come on, that was too slow—the goalie would have blocked that easily." "Don't try to kick that ball until you've stopped it!" "You've just got to belt those kicks if you ever expect to be a good soccer player." After one kick the boy, pleading for approval, asked, "Good kick, huh, Dad?" The father could not concede that it was, and grunted, "It could have been better."

Unfortunately, that well-intentioned father didn't know that improvement is grounded in success. Paul wrote to the Thessalonians: "We instructed you how to live in order to please God, *as in fact you are living*. Now we ask you and urge you in the Lord Jesus to *do this more and more*" (1 Thessalonians 4:1, emphasis added). Paul built on their past success to encourage further growth.

Therefore, in guiding the participation of your child, you should help him accumulate successes. Success will establish an "I can do it" attitude toward sports and, probably, toward other challenges.

But success should not be equated with stardom. Success comes from achieving one's goals. Your child might have the goal of making a team, or playing a certain number of minutes, or simply having fun. When I was a boy I played on a baseball team that was composed of Little League rejects. One of my teammates had two hitting goals. The first was to wrangle frequent walks—which he accomplished by concocting a number of weird stances to confuse the pitcher. The second was to make contact with the ball at least once during the season. That took longer—but eventually the ball and his bat occupied the same space, and he dribbled the ball to the infield. Our bench erupted with joy!

PARENTS AS INTERPRETERS

"Get it off my plate!"

"I've told you that you don't have to eat it. Just leave it on your plate, please."

"Oh, yuk! Get this off my plate. It's gross!"

"Son, that food won't contaminate anything else on your plate. Leave it there!"

"But I don't want it there. Take it off."

At that point my son begins to sob. The alien food is upsetting him terribly, and I can't convince him that the unwanted food is not poison in disguise. David Elkind, child development specialist, says that such irrationality is linked to children's inability to reason accurately. They aren't able to "think, reason, judge, and make decisions in the way that adults do. These capacities are developed in stages."[1]

1. David Elkind, *The Hurried Child* (Reading, Mass.: Addison-Wesley, 1981), p. 97.

The ability to interpret life accurately is fundamental to maturity. People are not shaped by their circumstances but by their interpretation of those circumstances. Two people lose their jobs. One believes that his heavenly Father will help him provide for his family. The other is overcome by worry as he listens to the unemployment statistics. As Christian adults, we have a reliable standard to judge the events in our lives. But learning to interpret life accurately (or biblically) comes in stages. It is dependent upon both spiritual *and* physical maturity. Young children, whether they are Christians or not, don't have the physical hardware to reason correctly. Young athletes' irrationality—which can take a variety of forms —can ruin their opportunities for success.

PERSONALLY RESPONSIBLE

Educational psychologist Robert Travers has discovered that preteen children believe they are solely responsible for their success or failure. Thus, when young athletes evaluate the outcome of a game, they don't factor in the play of their teammates, the decisions of coaches and referees, the skill of the other players, the weather, the condition of the playing field, or good fortune. They illogically attribute negative outcomes to personal deficiencies. (The same trait causes many children from broken homes to blame themselves for their parents' divorces.)

I am not suggesting that you teach your child to blame others for failure. Occasionally, it is good for a child to admit that his error or missed kick caused his team to lose. But he shouldn't be forced to accept blame always, or totally. When your youngster is disheartened from losing, remind him that he isn't totally responsible.

WINNERS ARE BETTER

Second, as previously mentioned, studies have found that children view winners as being better people. If losing is interpreted by the child as evidence of defective character, it will obviously be destructive to that child's self-image.

Parents, think about how you respond to your child's wins and losses. Are you enthused, complimentary, and happy when your child wins but silent, critical, and discouraged when he loses? If so, he may quickly learn that winning is fundamental to being a good child.

RIGID ASPIRATIONS

Mrs. Jones and her fifth-grade son, Johnny, approached me after a basketball game.

"Nice to see you here, Mrs. Jones. I've enjoyed having your son on the team. He's turned into quite a defender."

"Oh, I suppose. But I wish he was more aggressive. He often stands back when some of those other boys jump right in there." Johnny looked chagrined but said nothing.

"I wouldn't be too worried. He has made great progress. Look, my chart shows that he got five steals tonight. He wasn't getting more than one or two in our early games."

"Oh, I know. But—"

Unfortunately, many parents are unsatisfied with their child's performance. Research has found that parents maintain rigid aspirations in spite of their child's performance. They look at the best athletes and conclude that with more prodding or practicing their child will be a star. But sports psychologists point out that "elite athletes are born; they are not created out of common clay simply by hard training, the best coaching, or the most eager parents."

Our expectations should be tempered not only by our child's abilities but also by his rate of maturity. Success among a group of Little Leaguers was highly correlated with the timing of puberty. If parents *won't* recognize those differences, it will be extremely hard on the children—who, as we have seen, *can't* recognize the differences.

Of our two soccer playing sons, the eldest, Nathan, is quick and a good dribbler—skills that make him a leading scorer. When Andrew began to play he was frustrated because he wasn't matching his brother's exploits. But Andrew doesn't have the quickness to become a prolific scorer. His strengths are endurance and a strong leg. So I tried to convince him that his skills would make him a good defender. But the concept wasn't formed easily. One time Nathan came home from a game in which he had made two goals. He excitedly told the family how he had weaved through several defenders to make his goals. After listening to Nathan's explanation, Andrew whispered, "Dad, I'm not supposed to score goals, am I?" He needed reaffirmation—"No, Andrew, that isn't your job. It is your job to keep the other team from scoring." If our children are to enjoy sports, we must help them assess their talents accurately.

CONSISTENT PERFORMANCE

Some days my writing clicks. Thoughts fall naturally. Phrases come quickly. Editing goes smoothly. But other days the process is millstone-heavy. Thought is strained. Editing is continual. Progress is minimal.

Athletes are similar; they have good days and bad days. But many child athletes unreasonably expect to always perform at their peak. But such variables as a lingering cold, a strenuous bike ride, a worrisome family conflict, or a sore ankle make performances equally variable.

Don't let a poor performance overly discourage your child. It is a good opportunity to help him learn that imperfection is a part of being human.

The Parent as Encourager

The apostles gave Joseph from Cyprus a nickname —Barnabas, which means "Son of Encouragement." To encourage means "to inspire with courage, spirit, or confidence; to stimulate by assistance, approval." Because Barnabas was adept at building confidence and courage in others, he was dispatched to Antioch to nurture the first Gentile converts. He was also responsible for redeeming Paul and John Mark. Barnabas was a man who saw potential and offered support while the potential was being reached. He is a model for what many of our children desperately need.

A recent study found that child athletes want to perform well because they dread the disapproval of their parents.[2] Children are not full of confidence; they are full of fear. The following guidelines are designed to help parents inspire confidence in their sports-involved children.

PRAISE: INSPIRING CONFIDENCE

The best dribbler on the soccer team I coached was lightning fast. Next to him other kids looked like they

2. Ronald E. Smith and Frank L. Smoll, *Kidsports: A Survival Guide for Parents* (Reading, Mass.: Addison-Wesley, 1983), p. 39.

were standing still. The boy's father came to a game late, just missing a near goal by his son. As the boy ran by his dad, he called, "I almost made a goal, Dad." His father didn't smile. "But you didn't." I watched the boy's shoulders slump and his smile fade as he trotted back to midfield.

Why are so many parents unable to praise their children's achievements? Often they are concerned that their children will develop "big heads" if they overly praise them. But most often, the braggart's self-praise is a desperate and vain attempt to fill his need for approval—a need of all children, even the superstars.

What happens when children are continuously criticized? Drs. Carole and Russell Ames, professors at the University of Maryland, conclude: "Repeated experiences of this nature could conceivably contribute to a 'learned helplessness'—a belief that failure is inevitable and insurmountable because of one's low ability."[3] Chronic criticism does not spur a child on to greater achievements.

Unfortunately, one study found that parental fault-finding increases as children advance through sports.[4] It may be because of the greater investments required of parents. Chunks of time are devoted to shuttling kids to and from sports, to attending the games, to cooking extra meals, and to helping the child practice. Money is needed for equipment, lessons, and travel. As commitments increase, the parent may want a return on his investment.

---

3. Carole and Russell Ames, "The Thrill of Victory and the Agony of Defeat," *Journal of Research and Development in Education* 12, no. 1 (1978): 81.
4. P. Walley, G. Graham, and R. Forehand, "Assessment and Treatment of Adult Verbalizations at Youth League Baseball Games," *Journal of Sport Psychology* 4, no. 3 (1982): 264.

When the child doesn't perform well, the parent may become critical and demanding.

What is the best way for you to encourage your child? First, kids develop competence when their parents expect them to succeed. When you communicate to your child—"You can do it, Johnny! Come on, keep at it. You'll get it."—then he gains confidence in his performance.

Second, praise is most effective when you focus on specific skills. Rather than telling your child that he is a great basketball player, it is more helpful—and believable—to commend his passing or defending. Such selectivity helps him concentrate his efforts in one or two areas. A sense of competence comes from doing something —not everything—well.

BUILDING CONFIDENCE THROUGH PRACTICE AND TRAINING

Wise parents can find something to praise in their child—"I was sure impressed with the swing you made on that pitch." (It doesn't matter that he missed the pitch by a foot and, in fact, hasn't hit a pitch all season!)

But teammates and coaches are often less gracious. They want results. Practice and training can improve your child's performance and, therefore, the evaluation from others.

Practice—the source of improvement. You don't have to be a Larry Bird, Dan Marino, and Chris Evert Lloyd all rolled into one to help your child improve his skills. Just by being available to play catch or helping organize a backyard game you can hone his skills. Research has shown that successful athletes are the ones who have had the most opportunity to develop those skills. But be careful. On a recent soccer team we had a father who broke a rib and another who broke an ankle while practicing with their sons.

Training—the basis of peak performance. A few simple, age-appropriate training suggestions can improve your child's performance and the judgments of others. First, a child should have no more than three hard workouts per week—including games—because exercise mildly injures muscles. If kids alternate exercise and rest, their muscle tissue will be strengthened. Some coaches conduct a rigorous practice the night before a game and then wonder why their team lacks zip the next day. The muscles required more time to heal. Thus, if you want to maximize your child's performance, an activity like a long bike ride might be avoided on the day of a game.

Second, proper nutrition can enhance performance. Child athletes have two unique nutritional needs—they need more food and more water. The first—more food—can be met by three meals plus a couple of healthy snacks each day.

Regarding the need for liquids, there are dangerous misconceptions. When I was a boy, my coaches sternly warned us against drinking water during a game, reasoning that it would make us sluggish. We were only allowed to rinse our mouths. (It's amazing how much of that rinse water slid down our throats!) But water should not be denied. Enough perspiration to cause a child to lose as little as 2 percent of his weight can threaten his health by causing cramps, heat exhaustion, and even heat stroke. Young kids are especially vulnerable to overheating because they don't sweat efficiently. During hot weather, their games or practices should be shortened or rescheduled.

Finally, many erroneously believe that when we sweat we lose minerals that need replacement. Actually, mineral supplements (e.g., sports drinks or salt tablets) discourage an interest in water and may encourage overheating. But an ample supply of water should always be available during play.

BUILDING CONFIDENCE IN GIRL ATHLETES

Katherine Switzer, the first woman to run in the Boston Marathon, explained her feelings about competing in an earlier period of women's sports: "When I was running marathons, we were sailing on a flat earth. We were afraid we'd get big legs, grow mustaches, not get boyfriends, not be able to have babies. Women thought that something would happen to them, that they'd break down or turn into men."[5]

Though girls' participation in sports has mushroomed, they still suffer under the cultural view that "sports is a male sanctuary, therefore any woman who tries to invade it is not really a woman."[6] A friend's young daughter gave up soccer because her peers informed her that soccer was for tomboys.

Unfortunately, some Christians have supported the exclusion of women from sports, reasoning, "A woman's place is in the home." Does that mean that girls should be barred from sports? I think not. Watching my wife's joyous inauguration into soccer has convinced me that girls should be equally encouraged to compete. Cathy has enjoyed the exercise—though not the bruises. She has made new or better friends—in spite of a necessary confrontation with the "general" on her team. She has reveled in her own and her team's progress in gaining skills. Shoul-

5. Bob Abel and Mike Valenti, *Sports Quotes: The Inside View of the Sports World* (New York: Facts on File, 1983), p. 199.
6. Robert Lipsyte, *Sportsworld: An American Dreamland* (New York: Quadrangle, 1975), p. 217.

dering a commitment to her home does not conflict with an enjoyment of leisurely sports.

As recently as the 1930s it was thought that girls couldn't handle the physical and emotional stress of sports: "External stimuli such as cheering audiences, bands, lights, cause a great response in girls and are apt to upset the endocrine balance. . . . There is widespread agreement that girls should not be exposed to extremes of fatigue or strain either emotional or physical."[7]

But research has shown that sports harbor no special physical or emotional dangers for girls.

Some girls have been reluctant to participate, fearing that training will give them masculine-looking bodies. But women don't normally add muscle bulk in training.

The obstacles that discourage your daughter from participating in sports are not insurmountable if she has your support. Researchers have found that with the help of their parents—particularly their fathers—girls have been able to overcome the cultural barriers.

BUILDING CONFIDENCE IN THE UNATHLETIC CHILD

An uncoordinated child may find a walk through the house as dangerous as a walk through a mine field. It may be even more perilous for him to step on the ball field where winners are praised and losers are ignored or berated.

What can you do? First, take extreme care in choosing a sport. Avoid programs that place a heavy emphasis on winning or that don't give each child an equal opportunity to play.

Second, you must be realistic. Admit that your child will never be a star. But he can still enjoy sports. One

---

7. D. Stanley Eitzen and George H. Sage, *The Sociology of American Sport* (Dubuque, Iowa: William C. Brown, 1978), p. 272.

year my middle son had a boy on his soccer team who was terribly uncoordinated and unaggressive. During all the games I attended I never saw him actually kick the ball—unless someone slammed it into him. But that child has been blessed with a coach and a father who praise him if he gets his shoes on the right feet! The result is that he loves soccer.

THE PARENT AS OBSERVER

When our youngest son was three or four years old, he would continually complain, "I'm hungry. I'm hungry." Even a huge meal might be shortly followed by another chorus of "I'm hungry." We tried feeding him more often. We tried feeding him more. We tried different kinds of food. But nothing satisfied. Finally, we realized that the phrase was his childlike way of making known a host of needs—an "I'm hungry" might also be used to communicate ill health, boredom, tiredness, or a need for attention.

Children do expose their needs—but often in subtle ways. The following observational cues are designed to help you understand the sports-related needs of your child.

INJURIES

It is early in the basketball game. Eight-year-old Bill twists his ankle and must be taken out of the game. A little later he returns to the game but soon collides with a bigger boy and, once again, limps to the bench. The frequent injuries are a pattern for Bill. Is Bill more injury prone than other boys? Dr. James Garrick, the head of the division of sports medicine at the University of Washington, explained his attitude toward undetectable injuries in children: "[They mean] one of two things: (a) we're not smart enough to find the injury or (b) they don't want to play."[8]

Frequent injuries may be the child's way to communicate that he doesn't want to be playing. I believe that was the case with Bill, whose mother offered a loud critique of his performance from the sidelines. He found it safer on the bench than in the game.

STRESS

Stress is normal to sports. A child may have difficulty getting to sleep the night before a game or experience "butterflies." But stress is unwieldy when it causes a child to lose weight or to have prolonged sleeplessness or to quit sports or to continually perform below his abilities.

However, stress is only a signal. It is the *cause* of the stress that must be uncovered. Your child might be receiving onerous criticism from insensitive peers. He might have a coach who harshly corrects his players. There would be little gain in telling your child to relax unless you deal with the underlying causes.

Unfortunately, one study found that few parents are aware of the level of stress in their children. Apparently we are not reading their encrypted messages.

Social relationships. Sports can mirror a child's social skills. Watch the pre- and post-game interactions. Is your child included? Do the kids pester him or make fun of his abilities? When our son Andrew began playing sports, he was frequently—though playfully—punching and tackling other kids. After getting over my irritation, I recognized that he was uneasy in a new group of boys. I was

8. Thomas Tutko and William Bruns, *Winning Is Everything and Other American Myths* (New York: Macmillan, 1976), p. 139.

able to help him overcome that by inviting a couple of the boys over to play.

Achievement opportunities. One child plays the same video game over and over again. Another enjoys the challenge of a new game. One child is bored when his team wins all its games easily—another is overjoyed by being on a team that stomps its competition. What are these children demonstrating?

Children approach a challenge in two basic ways. They are either afraid of failure or they expect to succeed. The fearful child prefers tasks that are easy because they let him escape failure. The confident child chooses tasks that are moderately difficult because they provide a challenge.

Past experience determines a child's approach to a task. Success creates a willingness to venture into the threatening, middle ground of achievement. This child wants to succeed but also enjoys risk in its pursuit. He would be bored by sticking with the same video game. But the other child, who has experienced frequent failure, wants to avoid tasks that have an uncertain outcome. He would enjoy playing the same video game.

A fear of failure or an expectation of success is instilled into children at an early age, which, again, points to the critical nature of a child's early sport experiences. If your child appears to be afraid to fail (i.e., he chooses easy tasks), then you should intervene and help him experience success.

The Parent as Coach

The job description for coaching youth may seem overwhelming.

Hours:	Mostly evenings and weekends, 15-20 hours per week. Applicant must be willing to forgo vacations and other leisure activities.
Main responsibilities:	Develop character of, act as role model for, and improve sports skills in children.
Qualifications:	Someone with "perfect" patience.
Experience required:	None. (Those who have had experience normally don't re-apply!)
Pay:	Nothing.

But the commitment can pay large dividends— both for you and for the young kids who are developing their attitudes toward sports and achievement.

THE GOALS OF COACHING

Building relationships. In my first season as a soccer coach, I had a beginner who was a head shorter than the other boys. During the first game he was put in as a fullback to guard the goal. While play was going on at the other end of the field, the other fullbacks and the goalie entertained themselves by teasing and punching this young boy. He never returned.

I am now a wiser coach. I try to help the kids build good relationships with each other by accentuating the unique contribution of each child. For example, at the end of my oldest son's basketball season I gave ribbons to all the boys at a parent/son potluck. The awards stressed the individual's contribution to the team—"Most Steals," "Best Rebounder," "Most Improved Player," or "Best

Passer." I let the boys guess who would receive each award. They were right in most cases and genuinely enthusiastic about each other's awards. A team concept lessens the rivalry among children.

Some coaches try to motivate their teams by making the opponent look like gestapo agents! I try to counter the competitive tension between teams by phoning to compliment a coach on his team's improvement or by getting to know each of the other coaches by name or by sharing strategy with newer coaches. I have found that tension can be greatly reduced by such actions.

Encourage independence. A famous major-league baseball manager was quoted as saying, "I don't communicate with players. I tell them what to do. I don't understand the meaning of communication."[9] Is it any wonder that athletes have been found to be more dependent, conforming people? But it doesn't have to be that way. A study found that a group of young gymnasts was successful in self-training. Another study revealed that measures on children's creativity, motor skills, and self-image improved when they participated in decision-making.

While I was coaching a sixth-grade basketball team, the league suspended the rule requiring equal play for each player during a city tournament. But I decided to give the boys the choice. Did they want to play only their best—thus increasing the odds of winning, or did they want everyone to play equally? The boys voted to play their best players. As a result, the bench sitters were enthusiastic supporters of the better players during the tournament. The older kids get, the more they can participate in such decisions.

9. Abel and Valenti, p. 10.

Develop skills. Coaching involves more than patting kids on the back. As kids mature, their sense of competence is based more on actual performance. Therefore, improving children's skills will be an essential part of coaching. That takes a lot of work. When I began coaching soccer I knew more about nuclear physics than I did about soccer. But there are many books available for the beginning or advanced coach.

Help parents. This goal might be more accurately stated: "Survive parents!" I have a friend who coaches a youth baseball team. As he announced the lineup one night, a parent rushed up to him and said, "My son isn't going to play in the outfield. He's a second baseman." My friend calmly explained, "No, I have another boy who will play second base tonight." The parent was adamant. "No! My son is not going to play in the outfield. He has always played second base." My friend persisted—the boy played in the outfield.

Many volunteer coaches have not re-enlisted because of the behavior of parents. But most parents can be won to a child-centered philosophy of coaching.

You might begin the season with a letter explaining your philosophy of coaching. That can be followed by periodic memos reminding them to let you do the coaching, keep negative comments to themselves, avoid criticism of referees, and take time to practice with their child. Most parents are enthusiastic about such concepts.

Have fun. What do you suppose our cocker spaniel has added to (or should I say, subtracted from) a soccer scrimmage? As might be expected, he created the unexpected. His speed often made it possible for him to get to the ball before the kids could, but it was impossible to predict which way he would butt the ball. When he tired of tackling the ball, he started tackling the boys. I wanted to send him home, but the boys begged to let the fun continue.

Children's sports should be fun. In a culture that worships winning, it is important for a coach to ask whether his kids are enjoying themselves. Fun can be nurtured by letting kids scrimmage more, by watching the tone of your voice, by letting kids play a variety of positions, and by getting families together for team picnics. Championships can be won by only the few. Fun can be had by all.

Winning. Winning should be the last goal of the youth coach. Because sports were so important to me as a child, I have to be careful lest I get my ego involved in the team's win-loss record. When my teams have been in championship games, I have had to remind myself that the results aren't that important, that by next month no one will even care who won.

In the process of making winning a goal, it is important to help a team develop realistic goals. As mentioned, many children and adults rigidly maintain high expectations.

CONCLUSION

Dr. Terry Orlick tells about a friend, Cal Botterill, who organized a hockey team out of rejects from other teams. They began by setting their own goals.

> Botterill posed questions relating to why the boys wanted to play, what they wanted to accomplish, and how they might go about doing it. . . . The players talked things over and reached a consensus, sometimes

through voting. Once there was agreement, the team's basic objectives were distributed to the parents. The boys agreed upon equal play, equal time rule and there was no "static" about this by any parents, primarily because the players had set the rule.

The Eagles, as they came to be known, lost their first game 20-0. It's tough to find much to praise when a hockey team loses a game 20-0. However, by the use of specific short term goals relating to various behaviors and skills, such as knowing where to be on the ice, Botterill pointed out some legitimate areas of improvement. In practice, the players created some of their own drills, one of which was free skating across the rink, one by one, doing anything you could imagine, like hot dog skiing. They loved it!

By the middle of the season the team was "losing" by 12-4, better than last week. As the season moved toward a close, the Eagles finally did it, they accomplished one of their goals, they won a game—Eagles 2-Visitors 1. . . . All 15 boys who began the season were there to enjoy it. The Eagles had won!

A few years after the Eagles' debut, Botterill returned to the area where he had taught and coached and was pleased to find that a large percentage of these same youngsters were still playing hockey.[10]

That was obviously not Cal Botterell's first coaching experience. It takes time to develop such skills. But as can be seen from his story, it is worth the sacrifice.

THE PARENTAL ROLE: FINAL THOUGHTS

"Oh, I wouldn't think of missing one of Timmy's games. He would be disappointed if I wasn't there." Would he be that disappointed? Must a parent be at every game?

10. Terry Orlick, *Winning Through Cooperation* (Washington, D.C.: Acropolis, 1978), p. 152.

Be involved in your child's sport—but not too involved. At times, a vacation or a church retreat or the need of a friend might take precedence over a child's game.

Many kids have their primary contact with their fathers in sporting situations—playing catch, attending games, watching sports on TV. Teachers have told me that fathers seldom attend parent-teacher conferences, band concerts, or any school function—except sporting events. Fathers, if you do that, aren't you communicating that sports are supremely important? Since sports skills will not be primary in most adults' lives, we must give priority to the abilities that will serve our children a lifetime.

Furthermore, overly intense devotion to a child's sport may prevent parents from developing their own lives. Former champion swimmer Mark Spitz explained the difficulty his parents faced when his career was over: "[They] spent so much time devoting their attentions to my well-being, that I think they failed to devote enough attention to their own growth."[11]

Participation in sports is but one way that sports influence children. Children are also affected by such things as the popularity of athletes and the sports conversations of adults. The following section will deal with that broader yet more subtle influence.

11. Emily Greenspan, *Little Winners: Inside the World of the Child Sports Star* (Boston: Little, Brown, 1983), p. 77.

Part 3

The Sportsworld

7

The Sportsworld and Character

The devotion of Nebraskans to their football team is legendary. One fan labored to make his family's wardrobe reflect the team's color: "[We have] red in all weights of coats, all lengths of dresses, shirts, sports coats, slacks, jackets, shoes, boots, lined boots, hats, caps, scarfs, sweaters, shorts, ties, gloves, mittens, socks, watches, pins, bracelets, earrings, buttons. One cartoon showed a manufacturer who said, 'If it won't sell, paint it red and send it to Nebraska.' "[1]

Furthermore, football is a year-round occupation for Husker fans:

> We expect news coverage from August practice, through the fall season, including bowl practice in December and the bowl game in January. The balance of January and February are ugh. We look at the line-ups in March, follow spring practice in April and attend the spring Red-White squad game in May. Somehow we

---

1. James Michener, *Sports in America* (New York: Random, 1976), p. 220.

manage through June, but pro football with some former Big Red players starts in July, which carries us
back to August practice.[2]

How is this fan's child affected by his devotion? How
is an unathletic boy affected by the greater popularity of
athletic classmates? What impact does a father's commitment to televised sports have on his child? Those happen-
ings or events form a broad category of sports experience
that writer Robert Lipsyte calls the *sportsworld.*

The sportsworld refers to the aggregate of sports influence in our culture. It includes a child's participation
in sports as well as his exposure to sports through adult
or peer conversations, local athletic events, television, ra-
dio, bubble gum cards, books, cereal boxes, clothing
(with sports insignia), school pep rallies, newspapers,
speeches, and playground activities.

Why is a study of the sportsworld and its affect on
children important? First, because its influence is un-
avoidable. When a child plays on a softball team, he and
his parents control the decision to play or not. But the
influence of the sportsworld is not so easily avoided. Can
a child temper his father's zeal for the game of the week?
Can a child ask his peers to stop adulating good athletes?
Obviously not.

Second, a study is important because the sportsworld subtly, though effectively, communicates values to
our children. The ardent Nebraska fans, the children who
prize athletic ability, the father who is bound to the
TV—all of them are offering instruction in what is valuable. As Christian parents, we want our children to treasure a relationship with Jesus Christ. It is important for

2. Ibid., p. 220.

us to examine what effect the present saturation of sports may have on that relationship.

It is difficult to discuss the values of the sportsworld because the person or persons involved seldom hold those values consciously. When a father regularly chooses to watch a Sunday afternoon football game rather than play with his son, he doesn't consciously think, *Since this football game is more important to me than my son, I'll watch the game.* In fact, if the father were asked which was more important, the game or his son, he might become indignant—"What a stupid question!"

It is also difficult to talk about the values of the sportsworld because of its size and diversity. I have yet to hear of a meeting of the Sportsworld's Conference for the Establishment of a Unified Value System! Thus, my observations can never be applied universally.

Finally, there is the greatest difficulty—me! I have come to the subject with prejudice, with limited mental capacities, and with time constraints. Each limitation will certainly color my conclusions.

It is my contention that the sportsworld is having a weighty influence in the development of many children. The sportsworld projects a magnetic model of who kids should be (their character) and how they can invest their lives (their vocation). It is important to investigate those sportsworld models and compare them with the biblical model.

THE IDEAL ATHLETE

Chris Wood, while a senior end at Auburn University, praised his school's football program: "My mom sent her boy to Auburn, and Auburn sent her back a man."[3] A sur-

3. David Moore, "Auburn's Dye Not Ready to Relax Yet," *USA Today*, 5 Dec. 1983.

vey of parents revealed that 77 percent of them believe that sports has a positive effect on children.[4] But what is the effect—does sports build character—or characters? Before answering that question, it is necessary to look at the profile of the model athlete.

PERSISTENT

Persistence is the first trait stressed in the athletic world. Shortly after beginning his major league career, Mickey Mantle was demoted to the minor leagues. When he informed his dad he was thinking about quitting, he hoped his dad would say, " 'Oh, don't be silly, you're just in a little slump, you'll be all right, you're great.' But he just looked at me for a second and then in a quiet voice that cut me in two he said, 'Well, Mick, if that's all the guts you have I think you better quit.' "[5]

The number of slogans used to encourage persistence in sports indicates the relative importance of this trait: "When the going gets tough, the tough get going." "A winner never quits; a quitter never wins." "Never say die." "If at first you don't succeed, try, try again." The message is that the fruits of participation will be enjoyed by those who stick it out.

LOYAL

The ideal player is depicted as being loyal to the team and his teammates. When Dale Murphy won the Most Valuable Player award for the second straight time, he said, "I'm extremely honored and happy to share it

4. Tom Weir, "High School Sports Have a Place," *USA Today*, 28 Dec. 1983.
5. Mickey Mantle, *The Quality of Courage: True Stories of Heroism and Bravery* (New York: Bantam, 1964), p. 7.

with my teammates and coaches." The ideal athlete credits his success to others: "Oh, I'm just one player. I couldn't score all these points if it wasn't for the rest of the guys."

The player is also expected to be loyal to the coach by submitting to his guidance and his rules. The ideal athlete is the one who will "go through a wall" for a coach.

AGGRESSIVE

The third trait is aggressiveness. In baseball that is modeled by "Charlie Hustle," the ebullient Pete Rose. This trait is like persistence but adds exuberance and drive.

The aggressive person gives 110 percent. He strains as hard in practice as he does in games. He runs in situations where others might reasonably walk or jog. He labors to do his best whether the team is twenty points behind or twenty points ahead. He is often the crowd's favorite because he appears to make the most of his talent.

Rosalyn Sumners, the runner-up for the gold medal in figure skating at the 1984 Olympics, praised aggressiveness when she was asked what her greatest asset was: "It would be the determination, definitely determination and the want—you know, I want this and I'm going to do everything I can to get it—nothing's going to stop me. I feel that I also have great willpower and drive. The desire in me to win and always be the best is so strong. That's what keeps me pushing."[6] As Rosalyn said, the aggressive person is driven toward a goal and won't let anything hinder its fulfillment.

6. "Sumners Figures She Can Win Gold," *USA Today*, 19 Dec. 1983.

SELF-CONTROLLED

The fourth trait that is highly regarded in the sportsworld is self-control. Roger Staubach believed that his coach, Tom Landry, exemplified such impassability: "His self-control is amazing. I know he's been in moods or situations where he wanted to explode. But he wouldn't. His emotions stay inside. Tom controls himself better than any human being I've ever seen."[7]

The self-controlled athlete doesn't crack under pressure. In a tight golf tournament, he can rebound with a birdie after making a double bogey. In football, he is the quarterback who guides his team to a winning score in the final minutes of a championship game—not becoming distracted by a bad break or poor officiating or a mistake by himself or a teammate. He knows what he must do and controls himself so that he can concentrate on the task.

TOUGH

The final trait that the sportsworld emphasizes is toughness. Washington Redskins' coach Joe Gibbs praised his quarterback Jay Schroeder for playing with a cracked rib: "It was the greatest guts job I have ever seen."

Listen to sports on TV. Announcers will invariably praise someone for playing while he is injured. The ideal athlete is one who is tough, rugged. He is the one who doesn't bellyache about his hurts.

EVALUATING THE CHARACTER TRAITS

So what is wrong with persistence, loyalty, self-control, aggressiveness, and toughness? Obviously, nothing.

7. Roger Staubach, *Time Enough to Win* (Waco, Tex.: Word, 1980), p. 59.

We want our children to be able to complete a hard task. We want them to be loyal friends. We do not want them to passively depend on others. What then is the problem? The problem is one of definition and balance.

Definition is critical. For example, all Christians are in favor of evangelism. But what does it mean to evangelize? Evangelism does not mean that I harass my neighbor with invitations to attend church or that I witness to every unsaved acquaintance or that I explain the whole message of redemption each time. When such definitions are followed, the only fruit produced may be guilt. Thus, if we want our children to be loyal, for instance, we must ask, "Loyal to whom? Under what conditions?" In Nazi Germany many of the citizens—Christians included—hadn't learned that some authorities must be disobeyed.

The second concern is the issue of balance. When discussing the obligation to evangelize, a Christian's other responsibilities must be considered. What about prayer and study? What about the needs of others? Evangelism cannot dwarf all other tasks. Similarly, the character qualities stressed in the sportsworld must be laid within a biblical value system so they don't swallow other priorities.

PERSISTENT

Persistence is vital to the Christian life (cf. Hebrews 12:1-2). But what does it mean to be persistent? Can a person be *too* persistent?

Persistence and success. During the 1983 football season, SMU beat Texas A & M with a fourth quarter goal line stand. One of the defensive tackles explained: "It was just a matter of who wanted it more."[8] But was it strictly a matter of determination? Did their preparation make any difference? Were they just fortunate enough to guess where the Aggies would run the ball? Is it possible that they had more skillful players? Sportsworld messages often give the impression that persistence and success are faithfully bound in a monogamous relationship.

People can be ravaged by the belief that persistence will invariably lead to success. During the summer of my sophomore year in college, I took a job as a door-to-door book salesman. At sales school we were told that there are two kinds of men—those who find a way and those who make an excuse. Some would succeed that summer because they were determined to overcome any obstacles. Others would fail and justify it by making excuses about the weather or their territory or other factors. Those who ran the sales school drilled into us that hard work would guarantee success. But that was, at best, a half-truth. There were many factors that determined whether a salesman succeeded that summer. I was a "success" because I had a car and could cover more territory than those who didn't. I did well because I could socialize quickly with new people. I was successful because I had a good trainer. But few of us recognized those differences then. For the 25 percent who did not complete the summer, it was a shattering experience because they believed they lacked the guts to stick with it. Success requires more than persistence.

Persistence and quitting. When persistence is eulogized, it also distorts the definition of a "quitter."

8. N. Brooks Clark, "College Football Review," *Sports Illustrated* 59, no. 20 (25 Nov. 1983): 59.

"Winners never quit." Don't they? Of course they do. Ronald Reagan quit acting. The Wright brothers quit school to focus on their inventions. Peter quit fishing to follow Jesus. Leonard Koppett contrasted quitting in sports and in real life:

> In a baseball game, the rules guarantee each team the chance to score enough to win before making twenty-seven outs in nine innings. In life, the salesman's game may be over long before he realizes it, for any number of reasons: recession, racial prejudice, a poor product, body odor, whim, coincidence, unknown competition —anything. . . . In real life, the contestant must decide at which point he "still has a chance" and at what point he has embarked on a costly waste of time that might deprive him of other sales.[9]

Though God at times calls people to tasks where there is no apparent success (e.g., Jeremiah), quitting may be a mature response for the person who recognizes that God has better ways for him to invest his time.

Persistence and the complexity of life. Testimonies to persistence may support the delusion that success can be achieved by narrowly focusing one's energies. Don Shula praised his star quarterback Dan Marino as a man with "simple tastes and a simple goal—he wants to be the best quarterback in the NFL." But what about his marriage? What about his health? What about getting to know God? We call a businessman with a confined vision a workaholic. We call an athlete with such a focus dedicated.

But what is the price of such narrow diligence? Dick Radatz, a former major league All-Star, talked about his

9. Leonard Koppett, *Sports Illusion, Sports Reality: A Reporter's View of Sports, Journalism, and Society* (Boston: Houghton Mifflin, 1981), p. 189.

own quest for success: "Baseball is a single man's game. It kills family life. But a man's got to do what he's got to do. I had to persevere. I had to be a success."[10]

But does success mean that I sacrifice everything—even a marriage—in order to achieve a single goal? That is foolishness. Life is a process of juggling our roles as parents, husbands, wives, brothers, friends, workers. We don't have the luxury of indulging any part of our lives with exclusive attention. Persistence is needed in each area.

LOYAL

Any worthy character trait can be subverted. One coach believes that athletes' most valuable trait is "not physical ability but respect for authority." Is loyalty (i.e., respect for authority) really the most valuable? Such wild claims make it necessary to analyze the stress on loyalty.

Superficiality. When loyalty is overly stressed it may foster hypocrisy. Some athletes are asked to give a for-the-good-of-the-team message when deep inside they have contrary feelings. Jim Bouton was uncommonly honest in discussing his attitude toward his teammate during a spring training game:

> Jim O'Toole was pitching when I got there, and his curve wasn't sharp and he was walking a lot of guys. He's got about eight kids and spring training means more to him than a lot of other guys, but he was really laboring. I felt sorry for him, but not very.
>
> Let me explain. It was rather early to be playing an intrasquad game and I thought, "I hope nobody

10. Ed Kiersh, *Where Have You Gone, Vince Dimaggio?* (New York: Bantam, 1983), p. 224.

gets hurt." Then I had to amend that in my mind. I meant "I hope I don't get hurt." I've always wanted everyone to do well. But I don't want them to do well at my expense. Even when I was in junior high school, I'd sit there hollering encouragement and all the time I'd be saying . . . If he'd break his leg I could get in there and play." It's not exactly the perfect attitude, but it's the way I feel.[11]

No, that isn't the perfect attitude, but it is a common one that our athletic children will face. We must give kids the freedom to voice their genuine feelings rather than insisting on a superficial commitment to loyalty. Then we can help them learn the meaning of genuine loyalty.

Undiscerning obedience. There is a phrase in baseball that says, "He's a great guy. Never says a word."[12] But is that the response we want to encourage in our children? The Bible teaches that no human authority has the right to unquestioned allegiance. The Hebrew midwives disobeyed the pharaoh's command to kill Hebrew babies, and God rewarded them for their refusal. Shadrach, Meshach, and Abednego were forced to disobey the king's command to worship an image. Peter disobeyed the Jewish authorities and kept on preaching. Our children may face similar situations. In extreme cases, they may encounter an employer who asks them to break the law or a military officer who commands them to kill innocent women and children. More often they will face more subtle challenges to put their discernment to use. A clear

11. Jim Bouton, *Ball Four* (Briarcliff Manor, N.Y.: Stein & Day, 1981), p. 26.
12. Ibid., p. 110.

understanding of God's Word will be their best source of guidance.

Recently, my sons and I were riding bikes through a public park when the boys spied a tree full of apples. They scrambled up the tree and were in the process of filling their pockets when I heard a voice bellow, "Hey, you kids, get down out of that tree!" I turned to notice a park official heading our way. Uncertain as to whether the boys were actually in the wrong, I asked, "Is there a reason the boys shouldn't be picking apples?" He mumbled something about breaking some of the branches. I asked if it would be all right for them to pick if they were careful to stand on the strong branches. He sputtered a bit but eventually gave his OK. Sometimes those in authority just like to give orders, and often children are in a position where they have no choice but to obey. But I don't want my sons to give thoughtless obedience to anyone—not even to me. I, too, make mistakes and occasionally need my authority respectfully questioned. Obedience must involve discernment.

Dependence. Finally, too much stress on loyalty can create dependence in the athletes. For example, many college athletes submit to a regimen that includes being told when and what to eat, when and how to workout, when to study. Medical care is omnipresent. Tutors are more common than girl friends. Alumni arrange summer jobs. Such cradling is great—while it lasts. Ernie Banks, the former Chicago Cubs great, shares his adjustment to life outside sports:

> I didn't know how to deal with my environment, the real world. [My psychologist] helped me adjust, to get the right perspective on things. It's fabulous being a baseball star. But too many people direct your life.

You're always doing what you're told. This hurts you. Functioning later on is so difficult.[13]

Amazingly, the sportsworld claims that sports teach independence. A former NFL player says that obviously isn't true, because in college and professional games, players are still treated as adolescents: "They know . . . that you were never given a chance to become responsible or self-disciplined. Even in the pros you are told when to go to bed, when to turn your lights off, when to wake up, when to eat, and what to eat. You even have to live and eat together like you were in a boys' camp."[14]

Bob Hayes, former All-Pro for the Dallas Cowboys, was arrested on drug charges. In court, a psychiatrist described him as one who "lived a life under discipline, controlled and managed."[15] Loyalty to the sportsworld may produce individuals who are under control but not self-controlled.

Conformity. Loyalty becomes conformity when the rights of the individual are disregarded. An assistant football coach at Baylor University stated flatly, "The community expects a boy who's able to play to play. Football becomes important to him because it's important to the community." But why should community interests take precedence over the child's interests? As Glenn Dickey points out, such pressure tends to produce followers rather than leaders:

13. Kiersh, p. 6.
14. Thomas Tutko and William Bruns, *Winning Is Everything and Other American Myths* (New York: Macmillan, 1976), p. 40.
15. Wilbert M. Leonard II, *A Sociological Perspective of Sport* (Minneapolis: Burgess, 1980), p. 70.

When the demonstrations started at the University of California and football coach Ray Willsey bragged that none of his players were involved, possibly because he had nothing else to brag about at the time. He should have been ashamed of that, because it proved there were no leaders on the team, nor even any players who were thinking for themselves. The Cal student body, whether in favor of the demonstrations or opposed to them, was fervently aroused over the issue, but on the football team, passivity reigned. That was no surprise, because the system encourages reliance on others, usually coaches, for ideas and the very patterns of life. Conformity is the goal and conformists are not leaders.[16]

Conformity is the price athletes pay for their special treatment. A former NFL star, Lance Rentzel, talked about his response to such favors: "What you are to everyone is an extra special thing, and it scares you. To protect yourself, you learn to do what you are told. You do what they say . . . and they reward you. . . . Lots of accolades, publicity, approval, love."[17]

The pampered athlete is like the indulged child—his needs are met before they are detected. It is inconceivable to rebel against such constant, smothering care.

AGGRESSIVE

The aggressive person has the enthusiasm of a puppy. He nearly flattens you with a slap on the back. His handshake crunches your hand. He isn't feeling "Oh, all right"—he is feeling "Just great!" But when aggressive-

16. Glenn Dickey, *Jock Empire* (Radnor, Pa.: Chilton, 1974), p. 156.
17. Lance Rentzel, *When All the Laughter Died* (New York: Saturday Review, 1972), p. 64.

ness is stressed too much it can have a number of negative consequences.

Pace of life. The overly aggressive person views everything as a challenge, whether it is winning a world championship or beating a red light. At a press conference before the 1982 All-Star game, the following exchange was reported:

> "I never thought the object of the game was winning or losing," said [American League] catcher Carlton Fisk. "The idea is to honor players who excel at their positions. We're here to put on a show and to enjoy ourselves."
> Then Pete Rose stepped to the podium. "Losing stinks. You can't enjoy yourself unless you win."[18]

Isn't there a difference between a championship game and an all-star game? Between a friendly game of Monopoly and a professional game? What about an afternoon at the park? Could you enjoy yourself without organizing an active game? Could you hold your child in your lap and carelessly watch leaves settle onto a glassy pond? Unfortunately, probably not.

We measure the quality of life by its velocity. We think God has called parents to be recreation directors. We keep our kids involved, stimulated, entertained—all things that feed an aggressive "go, go, go" attitude. But when will we develop the quiet, meditative qualities that are fundamental to Christian maturity? The psalmist tells us: "When you are on your beds, search your hearts and be silent" (Psalm 4:4). But who can stay awake long

18. Sid Hartmann column, *Minneapolis Tribune*, 14 July 1982.

enough to do any silent searching after our exhausting schedules? The art of enjoying the unhurried things in life needs to be nurtured.

Public acclaim. The highly aggressive individual is addicted to new challenges. Old laurels provide little support. "The question is no longer: 'Did you win?' but 'How long are you going to keep winning?' Even if you are John Wooden and you win seven consecutive NCAA championships, your fans grumble when you fail to win an eighth."[19] No achievement can satisfy the hunger for success.

A performance focus (i.e., the need for recognition) may make it difficult to give time to private, unheralded activities such as family needs. Recently my sons and I were in a video arcade. A woman tapped me on the shoulder and said, "I just want you to know that it's neat to see a father who has fun with his kids." I was startled. Although strangers frequently commend my teaching abilities they seldom laud my parenting skills. But how often could they? Strangers don't see me take time at bedtime to read and talk with my sons. They don't see me prepare for family worship. They don't know about the times I get up to help my youngest to the bathroom. (I must confess that on this count, my motives are less than perfect—it is easier to take my son than to wake my wife!) Many of our actions have few witnesses. Fortunately, we have a Father "who sees in secret" and who will reward us for faithfulness in the unglamorous, unseen, but not unimportant duties in life. If the go-getter is motivated by public acclaim, he will have a difficult time being faithful in such areas.

19. Tutko and Bruns, p. 2.

SELF-CONTROLLED

Self-control has been meagerly defined as a lack of emotional display. We train our children—especially our sons—to ignore their feelings. A scene I frequently witness was repeated at a recent soccer game. An eight-year-old boy had the soccer ball slammed into his face. He slumped to the sidelines, crying and seeking comfort in his mother's arms. But she was more embarrassed than compassionate, and chided him saying, "Now, I know it hurt, but I don't think it hurt that much." The boy continued bawling for the next thirty minutes—he was determined to convince his mother that it really did hurt! Had she offered genuine comfort, the child would have probably returned quickly to the field.

It is healthy to express emotion. Jesus was enraged over the Jews' abuse of the Temple. He shed tears at the death of a friend. He was frustrated by people's lack of faith. He agonized and pleaded with God to find an alternative to the cross. A lack of emotion is not a sign of maturity.

Repression doesn't work. Attempting to conceal emotions doesn't remove them. During a counseling session, a young woman explained her frequent tears as "just being silly." Her husband explained, "She's just being a woman." But silliness and womanhood aren't enough to account for frequent crying. Their attitude suggests a misunderstanding about emotions. The parent who says, "Big boys don't cry," or, "Don't you get angry with me!" forces the child's feelings underground where they will thrive unconsciously. Genuine self-control is only possible when the emotions are brought into the light where they can be confronted and understood.

But how frequently do athletes divulge their emotions? Imagine attending a sports banquet and hearing an aging professional reveal his insecurity as he watched younger athletes replace veterans on the team. Or imagine a coach honestly confronting the fear of getting hurt on the football field. Because those emotions are seldom discussed, many young athletes believe their feelings are unique. But Crites and Fitzgerald reported that the "fear of failure permeates the adolescent life of the young male —in school, in sports, in social relations."[20] Trying to deny emotion is like trying to squeeze air out of an air mattress —it keeps popping up in a different place.

Genuine self-control is evidenced not by a lack of emotional display but rather by the way athletes treat referees, erring teammates, or a critical press.

TOUGH

An athlete has to endure hardship before he can become a champion. He logs hours of training and battles recurring injuries. He must be strong if he hopes to reach his goal. However, when toughness is overdeveloped, it may discourage the tenderness and vulnerability that are fundamental to relationships with God and others.

A relationship with God. A relationship with God is built on weakness. Paul said, "If I must boast, I will boast of the things that show my weakness. . . . so that Christ's power may rest on me" (2 Corinthians 11:30; 12:9). As with Paul's thorn in the flesh, our defects are continuing reminders of our need for God. A recent study of Matthew 6 reminded me that I am frequently hounded by "the worries of this life." I recorded my worries and

20. John Crites and Louise Fitzgerald, "The Competent Male," in *Counseling Men*, eds., Thomas Skovholt, P. Schauble, and R. Davis (Monterey, Calif.: Brooks-Cole, 1980), p. 44.

took the list to God: "Lord, thank You for this recurring problem of worry that leads me to dependence on You." It would be interesting to meet with a group of Christian friends and spend time bragging about our weaknesses. It could be a tremendous time of worship as we praised our heavenly Father for the needs that led us to rely on Him.

I had a recent discussion with a man who ministers to athletes. He said that one of the main obstacles to his ministry is the athletes' indifference. He believes it is caused by a lack of felt needs. It isn't that athletes aren't needy—everyone is desperately needy. But the sportsworld has taught athletes to feign strength by denying weakness. Joe Namath reported Bear Bryant's response to a teammate's dislocated finger: "Nobody ever died of a . . . broken finger!" Some say that men are tough; they can handle their problems. But true strength comes through admitting inadequacy. "I can do everything *through him* [Christ] who gives me strength" (Philippians 4:13, emphasis added).

A relationship with others. When people are cloaked with strength, they won't seek help. Johnny Blanchard, a New York Yankee during the 1960s, tried to maintain the masquerade in spite of a drinking problem: "You can't talk to anyone about it, it's too macho a world. You have to maintain your manhood, and a conspiracy of silence develops."[21]

Like Blanchard, many men still childishly insist, "Let me do it myself!" But the New Testament's concept of the Body of Christ is that "the body is not made up of one part but of many" (1 Corinthians 12:12). Just as one part of a physical body can't exist without its members, so the spiritual body can't either. Eyes need hands. Feet need legs.

21. Kiersh, p. 205.

Though men may appear to have more friendships than women, those friendships lean toward superficiality. As the quarterback on his high school football team, Gary Warner spent hours working on the timing of the snap with his center. He said, "How many snaps did [Bill] give me? Thousands, but I never knew Bill. Never knew what he dreamed about or hurt about or cared about."[22]

Nurture and comfort must be received before they can be given (see 2 Corinthians 1). One study discovered that more than 50 percent of a group of men could not remember being hugged by their fathers.[23] It isn't a sign of debility for a boy or a man to be affectionate. Jesus was the perfect man. He touched lepers, snuggled children in His arms, and let a sinful woman kiss His feet.

The athletic world, by stressing a show of strength, may discourage athletes from establishing the relationships that mend broken people.

CONCLUSION

The inadequacy of the character traits stressed in the sportsworld has been discussed. Two general deficiencies of the sportsworld's model will be analyzed in conclusion.

THE EXCLUSIONS

I once asked an elderly woman what she would have done differently as a parent. She said that she and her husband had pondered that question and concluded that their major faults were not in what they did but in what they didn't do. The sportsworld has the same problem

---

22. Gary Warner, *Competition* (Elgin, Ill.: David C. Cook, 1979), p. 99.
23. R. Lewis, "Emotional Intimacy Among Men," in Skovholt, Schauble, and Davis, p. 85.

—its exclusions are the cause for concern. It seldom emphasizes "love, joy, peace, patience, kindness, gentleness."

But must the sportsworld disseminate all the values? Can't it emphasize some while children absorb others in their home, church, or school? No, it can't. Values are never communicated in isolation. When a coach tells his athletes that their "most valuable characteristic" is "respect for authority," he is not simply lecturing on the *need* for respect but also the *priority* of respect.

Jesus' priority system began with love—a love for His Father and a love for others. Whether we are fathers, mothers, or coaches, a principal concern should be the care of others.

Some coaches justify aloofness with their players by stressing the need for objectivity. Roger Staubach explained why he didn't become an intimate friend of his former coach and fellow believer Tom Landry:

> Keeping our distance was the best way to maintain a respectful coach-quarterback dialogue. Socializing together wouldn't work because of the demands each of us faced. He had to tell me about my play, and sometimes what he had to say wasn't favorable. I had to be open with him, even if it meant saying I didn't think the last play he called was so hot.[24]

Is that a right attitude? Can't friends be honest about the other person's failings? Imagine a parent saying, "I didn't want to get close to my kids because I was afraid it might affect my judgment." Obviously, intimacy affects one's judgment—but it is usually for the better. We simply have not thought clearly about what it means to be a

24. Staubach, p. 69.

loving friend in the sportsworld. How can a coach balance the individual's needs and the team's needs? How can an athlete love a teammate with whom he is competing for playing time? How can a Christian be encouraged to love his opponents?

I don't mean to suggest that there aren't athletes who are committed to loving others. The problem is that the sportsworld gives so little attention to love.

THE DEFINITION OF MANHOOD

One of the most serious threats to the development of boys takes place when those involved in the sportsworld equate manhood with the athletic model.

A few years ago, CBS vividly portrayed the rugged life of a professional football player. At one point the athlete turned to the camera and said, "Professional football is for men, not boys." Pepper Rodgers, a former coach at Georgia Tech, said that boys growing up in the South "have to play football to be accepted as a man."[25] It is often the same throughout the country—a seventh-grade boy of a friend of mine was called a "sissy" by his peers because he didn't go out for the school football team. The message is clear—a boy can prove his masculinity by being an athletic star.

Some coaches exploit the manhood-through-sports myth to get a maximum effort out of their athletes. Gary Shaw believed that his coach, Darrel Royal, was successful because he played on the fears of his players. It was "their fears of masculinity, their fears of acceptance, their fears of not being good enough—in short, their need to feel like acceptable men. . . . We were trying to prove ourselves as men and we wanted approval from an au-

25. Tutko and Bruns, p. 66.

thority that we'd passed the test. And Royal held the cards of approval."[26]

One journalist said that Vince Lombardi's success came from treating a group of men like high school boys. Willie Davis, a star for Lombardi, explained what motivated him: "We went out and we whipped them good and preserved our manhood."[27]

Gary Shaw points out that making athletics a rite of passage to manhood even corrupts the winners.

> Anytime other players were treated with a total lack of concern, we had to justify this by either ignoring it or accepting the idea that our friends were losers. . . . For [us] to believe in this system of male winners made it practically impossible not to think of [ourselves] as. . . . superior—real men.[28]

But an even more serious result than the haughtiness of the winners is the brokenness of the losers. For those boys it can be a world "full of hatred and violence which is expressed mostly against the self."[29] Boys who fail in the sportsworld are made to feel like failures in life.

Parent, your child must know that sports can never establish a lasting identity. Paul's prescription for an insecure Timothy was: "Train yourself to be godly. For physical training is of some value, but godliness has value for all things, holding promise for both the present life and the life to come" (1 Timothy 4:8). Sports have "some value," but a child's most vigorous training should be for

---

26. Gary Shaw, *Meat on the Hoof: The Hidden World of Texas Football* (New York: St. Martin, 1972), p. 207.
27. Donald F. Sabo and Russ Runfola, eds., *Jock: Sports and Male Identity* (Englewood Cliffs, N.J.: Prentice-Hall, 1980), p. 85.
28. Shaw, p. 111.
29. Peter Stein and Steven Hoffman, "Sports and Male Role Strain," in Sabo and Runfola, p. 69.

godliness. Learning how to give and forgive, learning how to comfort and assist, learning how to study and pray —those are the tasks that should define who your child is and how he measures up—not what he does in sports.

8

The Sportsworld and Vocation

The Los Angeles Lakers are close to thwarting the Boston Celtics in their quest for another championship. With the Celtics trailing by twenty points in the third quarter of the final game, an exasperated Bill Russell slams his hands together in a "T" to signal for a time-out.

When the players arrive at the bench, Coach Red Auerbach initiates a last-ditch strategy for his tired and dejected players. "Men, you know we've had this rookie who has hardly played all year. We've tried everything. I'm going to give him a chance." The players give him a look of disbelief.

As the rookie pulls off his warm-ups, there is a deep groan from the 15,000 fans jamming the Boston Garden. The loudspeaker announcement that Bernie Schock will play guard is met with a chorus of boos. Can Auerbach be that desperate?

The first time down the court the rookie shoots a twenty-footer that misses completely. The boos become louder—some directed at Auerbach, the majority at the obviously nervous rookie. But the rookie begins a silent pep talk. "Come on, Schock, you can do it. You know you can."

The newcomer has the awesome task of guarding the tricky Elgin Baylor. The Lakers quickly get the ball to Baylor, who spins, dips, goes up for the shot, but what has happened? The rookie has stolen the ball and is streaking up court for an easy basket. The crowd's booing stops.

Baylor again tests the rookie with one of his slippery moves. But this time the rookie stuffs the ball in his face. Russell picks it up and throws it to the breaking Havlicek for another basket. The fans begin to nudge each other.

After the Lakers miss again, Havlicek passes to the rookie who arches a long shot toward the basket—*swish!* The crowd is on the edge of its seat. Immediately the rookie steals a Laker pass and feeds Russell for a dunk shot. The twenty-point lead is now twelve. The fans are hysterical. They can't believe that this rookie has turned the game around. He goes on to play a sensational game leading the Celtics to victory.

Obviously, that game never took place—except in my driveway. It was the arena in which I could achieve a plasticized model of the athletic success I so desperately sought. Sports as a profession is widely appealing. Joe Kapp, former All-Pro quarterback in the NFL, said, "If I ask kids who wants to be President, I might get one hand up. But when I ask them who's going to play for the 49ers, they all raise their hands."[1] Why are professional sports so highly valued? As Christian parents, two of our primary concerns are our children's character development and their vocational choices. The previous chapter evaluated the sportsworld's impact on children's character.

---

1. Glenn Dickey, *Jock Empire* (Radnor, Pa.: Chilton, 1974), p. 208.

This chapter will evaluate the dream of playing sports professionally.

Are children's dreams important? Research discovered that daydreams have a greater impact on occupational choice than the individual's talents.[2] Thus, kids who make a sports career their chief dream may pursue it over their natural abilities. Jim Bouton explained his efforts to make a comeback in the major leagues: "There's no use asking me why I'm here, why a reasonably intelligent thirty-year-old man who has lost his fastball is still struggling to play baseball, holding on—literally—with his fingertips. The dreams are the answer. They're why I wanted to be a ballplayer and why I still want to get back on top again."[3]

The Appeal of Professional Sports

The desire to play sports professionally seems to be motivated by opportunities for pleasure, achievement, freedom, recognition, and comfort.

PLEASURE

As a boy, each spring I played softball during my lunch hour. As noon approached, I began to put away my books in anticipation of charging out the door. I made a mad dash home on my bicycle, gulped down a sandwich, and made an equally mad dash back to the school grounds. With Mom's help—she had the crucial role of having lunch on the table—I could accomplish all that in under fifteen minutes! During those days I thought, *What could possibly be greater than playing this game to make my*

---

2. James Morgan and Thomas Skovholt, "Using Fantasy and Daydreams in Career Counseling," in *Career Counseling: Theoretical and Practical Perspectives*, ed. Stephen G. Weinrach (New York: McGraw-Hill, 1979), p. 136.
3. Jim Bouton, *Ball Four* (Briarcliff Manor, N.Y.: Stein & Day, 1981), p. x.

living? Many children would agree when they hear an athlete such as Kurt Rambis, a Los Angeles Laker forward, claim that he has "the greatest job in the world."

ACHIEVEMENT

Everyone needs to feel competent at something. Many have found that sense of achievement through sports. Novelist James Michener gave this tribute to sports: "If there was ever an American boy who was saved by sports, it was I. . . . We won championships and I came to regard myself as a champion. I carried myself a little taller, worked a little harder in school, built a confidence that was crucial."[4]

The child who has had his achievement needs met in sports may hope to have his adult needs for achievement met similarly.

FREEDOM

Juan Pizzaro, major league pitcher from the 1950s to the 1970s, enjoyed the freedom of his profession: "I didn't have to get up at six in the morning and go to work. I could just lie around all day, get me some pizza, or corned beef sandwiches, and then think of getting to the ballpark."[5]

Professional athletes have freedom from the nine-to-five schedule. Their seasons last six to eight months. Their games and practices last only two to three hours. When compared to clock punchers, they seem to have a carefree existence.

4. James Michener, *Sports in America* (New York: Random, 1976), p. 5.
5. Ed Kiersh, *Where Have You Gone Vince Dimaggio?* (New York: Bantam, 1983), p. 135.

RECOGNITION

An aging Jim Bouton was honest about why he was trying to hang on in the major leagues: "I enjoy the fame of being a big-league ballplayer. I get a tremendous kick out of people wanting my autograph. In fact, I feel hurt if I go someplace where I think I should be recognized and no one asks me for it."[6]

There are few professions that offer as much potential acclaim as that of the professional athlete. In contrast, a business man may have to wait until he receives his twenty-five year pin before his company extols his contribution. The desire for recognition may fuel children's desire to make sports a career.

FINANCIAL SECURITY

Magic Johnson's contract with the Lakers earns him a million dollars a year for twenty-five years. Golfer Jack Nicklaus has used success in golf to become a multimillionaire. Sugar Ray Leonard earned 17 million dollars in his two fights with Roberto Duran. A professional football player's average salary is more than $90,000. Basketball is even more lucrative, with salaries more than $200,000 per season. Those figures don't even include other sources of sports-related income. In 1980, Bjorn Borg made about 2 million dollars on his tennis ability and 3 million on his name.

We live in a society that has convinced us of our "need" for new cars, bigger homes, and lavish vacations. The sportsworld appears to provide a route to the resources needed to gratify those desires. In discussing the present-day atmosphere of youth sports, one writer said,

6. Bouton, p. xx.

"The dream of excellence is now partly a dream of striking it rich."[7]

EVALUATING THE APPEAL

Dorothy made a long, perilous journey to the Emerald City under the assumption that the Wizard of Oz could return her to Kansas. She was shocked when she found that the "great and powerful Oz" was nothing but a hoax. Fortunately, that story is a fantasy, and the writer had another solution to Dorothy's dilemma.

The sportsworld is also a fantasyland that cannot fulfill the dreams of most kids. But once there, no author can grant their dreams with a stroke of the pen. The following evaluation is designed to uncover the fantasy.

PLEASURE

The life of the professional athlete is not unending ecstasy. Few professions are so bare to scrutiny. In football, a quarterback is rated against his contemporaries —and his predecessors—by statistics on completions, interceptions, touchdowns, and total yards. Would homemakers appreciate similar treatment? "Thank you for joining us on WSOK for the ' "SOK" It to You' program. Today we will invade the kitchen of Cathy Schock. We have found that in the past year 5.4 percent of her cakes were burned, 3.7 were gooey, and 4.8 lacked one of the main ingredients. While 25 percent were judged 'superior,' an astonishing 32 percent were judged 'poor.' This puts Mrs. Schock in the lower third of baking mothers in this country." Ridiculous? Of course, but not far from the experience of professional athletes.

7. Emily Greenspan, *Little Winners: Inside the World of the Child Sports Star* (Boston: Little, Brown, 1983), p. 223.

The seeming pleasure of playing professional sports must be contrasted with the intense pressure to make and stay on the team. One veteran NBA player remembered the stress: "I look around and see those rookies all worried about what they have to do to make it. I remember it, oh man, it's awful. It's the worst pressure there is."[8] But there is little relief once a player makes the team. As baseball's former MVP Dale Murphy has said: "In this game, if you're doing something right, you need to do it every year." How would a businessman feel if every year his boss held tryouts for his job? Or how would a wife feel if her husband gave yearly tryouts for her job? The realities of the professional world often wring the joy from the games.

ACHIEVEMENT

Kids may dream about having their achievement needs met through sports, but the odds are slim. Of the millions who play youth basketball, for example, only 700,000 play as high school seniors. By the time those boys are college seniors, only 15,000 are still playing. Of those 15,000, only 200 are drafted by professional teams, and 50 make a pro team. Thus, a boy has about a 1 in 14,000 chance of playing professional basketball. The odds are similar in other sports.[9]

Even for the fortunate few who fulfill their dreams, their careers will never outlast their need for achievement. Even the Gaylord Perrys and the George Blandas retire long before most people. James Michener observed,

8. Blaine Johnson, *What's Happenin'?* (Englewood Cliffs, N.J.: Prentice-Hall, 1978), p. 32.
9. Ronald E. Smith and Frank L. Smoll, *Kidsports: A Survival Guide for Parents* (Reading, Mass.: Addison-Wesley, 1983), p. 205.

"In their middle thirties these gifted men had reached the climax of their fame." Most pro athletes are forced to retire at an age when Michener, in his profession, had not written a single word!

Some athletes have recognized that they will need new challenges when their careers end—but most have given the future little thought. The problem is that thinking too much about their uncertain futures may add pressure on them to maintain their athletic performance. Thus, they have tended to lose themselves in the comforting discipline of their sport. It is a place where "they can avoid making complex decisions, they can narrow the focus of their lives, they can avoid their responsibilities as husbands, lovers, fathers, sons, citizens."[10]

The dashed dreams of athletic success may be the seeds of the overly zealous fan. Fans "maintain their intense identification [with sports stars] because it serves as a method of resolving anxiety that was generated by the overblown expectations."[11] As a victim of such expectations, I can identify with a fan whose child was about to be born:

> My wife's labor increased in frequency and intensity; obviously it was time to go to the hospital.
>
> I warmed up the car but had not turned off the T.V. Detroit and Montreal were playing hockey. Joyce was at the door, beckoning. I turned for one last look. It was late in the third period. The score was tied and Detroit had a power play.
>
> "Just one more rush, honey," I said. "Just one more rush . . ."

10. Robert Lipsyte, *Sportsworld: An American Dreamland* (New York: Quadrangle, 1975), p. 16.
11. Richard Lipsky, *How We Play the Game* (Boston: Beacon, 1981), p. 126.

She gaped at me unbelieving. I don't believe it
either . . . now.[12]

Unrealistic hopes of accomplishment through professional sports may harbor that kind of vicarious fulfillment.

FREEDOM

I am relaxing in our sun room in January watching a
pro golf tournament. My mind is confused by the contrast
between the warm, summery scene on my TV and the
cold, icy look out my window. The announcer informs me
that the players are playing for more than $500,000 in
prizes—the winner will pocket $90,000. I begin to dream.
What could be greater than playing a few rounds of golf
each weekend to make a living? Jack Stirling, a PGA official, explained the realities: "The ideal training process
means hitting about 600 balls a day. That means . . .
swinging a club every 45 to 60 seconds and doing it for
four hours in the morning, breaking for lunch, then another four hours in the afternoon—day after day."[13]
The rigorous training for swimmers led Mark Spitz
to conclude: "Swimming is too demanding. It's also boring. You work six or seven hours a day just so you can
splash water faster than anyone else. There's gotta be
something more to life."[14] Tennis champion Billie Jean
King talked about the mixed blessing of the expanded
tennis tour: "The pro tours have created a great opportunity for all of us, to win money and destroy our bodies at

12. Gary Warner, *Competition* (Elgin, Ill.: David C. Cook, 1979), p. 1.
13. Wilbert M. Leonard II, *A Sociological Perspective of Sport* (Minneapolis:
    Burgess, 1980), p. 51.
14. Bob Abel and Mike Valenti, *Sports Quotes: The Inside View of the Sports
    World* (New York: Facts on File, 1983), p. 177.

the same time."[15] What appears to be a free, unstrained life is often quite different.

RECOGNITION

Mark Spitz was awed by the recognition he received: "I had never imagined all the attention I would get. It was mind-boggling."[16] But praise can turn quickly to censure.

The fan's attitude is often depicted by the saying, "What have you done for me today?"—with the emphasis on *today*. The fickle attitude of fans was difficult for former NBA player George McGinnis to adjust to: "From the time I started playing, all I heard was how well I played. . . . It was almost as if I were superhuman. . . . Then we went to the NBA championship, and when we lost, I was blamed. . . . I took it to heart. It was the first time I heard terrible things written and said about me."[17] One player acridly described his fans as people who would "boo funerals, an Easter egg hunt, a parade of armless war vets, and the Liberty Bell."[18] The adulation of athletes lasts no longer than their skills. The fickle fan will quickly turn his allegiance elsewhere.

FINANCIAL SECURITY

There are two problems with what the sportsworld communicates about money. First, it may further the notion that money is the avenue to the good life. While my wife and I were living in Florida, we often saw an advertisement enticing couples to cruise the Bahamas in a

15. Greenspan, p. 269.
16. Ibid., p. 275.
17. Woodrow Paige, Jr., "McGinnis, Out of NBA, Accepts the Truth," *Minneapolis Tribune*, 5 Dec. 1982.
18. Bob Chieger, *Voices of Baseball: Quotations on the Summer Game* (New York: Atheneum, 1983), p. 39.

rented yacht. The ad displayed beautiful sunsets, smiling faces, calm seas, and refreshing dips in the ocean. I began to fantasize about what an idyllic vacation Cathy and I could have for $2,500. But it was mostly fantasy. The ad didn't show anyone suffering seasickness. It didn't mention that problems in a relationship don't evaporate in an ideal setting. The ad didn't say that boat engines sometimes break down, that storms can be dangerous, or that people get sunburned. For $2,500 we could have cruised on a yacht in the Bahamas, but that would not have guaranteed an enjoyable vacation.

No, happiness cannot be bought. But ostentatious athletes may communicate just the opposite. Tennis star Vitas Gerulitas, "who has flowing blond locks and a vast array of high fashion clothes and high class ladies, loves his gaudy bachelor life style. 'You only live once,' he says, 'and you better smell the roses while you can.' "[19] But there is a surer way for the wealthy to find real life: "Command them to do good, to be rich in good deeds, and to be generous and willing to share. In this way they will lay up treasure for themselves as a firm foundation for the coming age, so that they may take hold of the life that is truly life" (1 Timothy 6:18-19).

The second lie nurtured by the sportsworld is that money is readily available. Kids' perceptions of the potential payoff are warped because they never get the viewpoint of those who fall short. Jim Bouton described what greeted him when he was demoted to the minors: "The locker stalls are made of chicken wire and you hang your stuff on rusty nails. There's no bat rack, so the bats, symbolically enough, are stored in a garbage can. There's no air-conditioning and no heat, and the paint on the

19. Lipsky, p. 119.

walls is peeling off in chunks. . . . The minor leagues are all very minor."[20]

But even if athletes make big money, their paychecks can be eroded by agents, accountants, lawyers, and taxes. *Golf Digest* estimated that a professional golfer who makes $90,000 a year would have a take home pay of just $31,000.

CONCLUSION

It is not enough to expose the sportsworld vision. Our children need dreams that will capture their hearts and direct their futures. The following section will discuss how biblical values can be passed on to our sports-influenced children.

20. Bouton, p. 121.

Part 4

The Spiritual World

9

Values and Visions: Serving the Kingdom

Now for the hard part. Fault-finding is easy, but it is more difficult to pass on biblical truth. This chapter will synthesize what we hope to develop, rather than avoid, in our sports-influenced kids.

Kingdom Values

Values are the skeleton upon which character is hung. Our children's character will be strong if we pass on the values of the eternal kingdom.

THE TWO GREATEST COMMANDMENTS

There are two priorities that stand apart—a love for God and a love for man (Mark 12:29-31). Parents, can you honestly say that your love for God is *the* controlling influence in your life? In Texas, high school football is king. It is "discussed in churches . . . cafes, schools, Kiwanis club meetings, oil fields and out on the north forty. Foot-

ball, particularly high school football, is the staff of life."[1]
Think about it. What do you get most enthused about? Do
you drag your feet to church but rush home to catch the
opening kickoff? Remember, your child's devotion to God
will be a reflection of your devotion.

Loving God should result in loving what He loves.
James asked: "Has not God chosen those who are poor in
the eyes of the world to be rich in faith and to inherit the
kingdom he promised those who love him?" (James 2:5).
But our tendency is to love the lovely. When my eleven
year old's basketball team lost their fifth straight game,
he complained to me about several unskilled teammates.
I was the team's coach and was able to say to him, "I
know you're disappointed, Nathan. Sometimes I too wish
that we had more skillful players. But think about it—if
they were on another team they might not play much and
might be heavily criticized." Nathan didn't jump up and
down and say, "You're right, Dad. I sure am glad we have
such lousy players." But it did provide a model of God's
priority on people.

THE NATURE OF SUCCESS

The Bible defines success differently than the sportsworld does. First, it has a different view of losing. NFL
coach Don Shula said, "No one ever learns anything by
losing."[2] Don't they? The apostle Paul summed up the
biblical view: "We also rejoice in our sufferings, because
we know that suffering produces perseverance; perseverance, character; and character, hope" (Romans 5:3). Losing can be a powerful instrument for personal growth.

Second, biblical success is well-rounded. When a

1. Richard Lipsky, *How We Play the Game* (Boston: Beacon, 1981), p. 81.
2. D. Stanley Eitzen and George H. Sage, *The Sociology of American Sport* (Dubuque, Iowa: William C. Brown, 1978), p. 67.

church selects leaders it does not find a person who is skilled with money, another who is a gifted teacher, and another who is hospitable. A church leader must be *all* that and more. Success in our culture is more constricted. Athletes who break records and businessmen who make gobs of money are considered successful—it usually doesn't matter whether they are abominable spouses, parents, or friends.

Finally, biblical success is equated with faithfulness (1 Corinthians 4:2). In writing this book I am employing God-given time, talents, and resources. But I don't control the "success" of this book. I can't influence the buying habits of parents. Likewise, a young athlete is successful when he is faithful and lets God control the results.

THE CONTRIBUTION OF THE INDIVIDUAL

As children age, sports opportunities become limited. There are fewer teenagers in high school sports than in junior high sports. There are fewer college athletes than high school athletes. But it isn't just in sports that children feel excluded. Only a few win scholarships. Only a handful become homecoming kings and queens. That discrimination makes many kids feel unimportant.

The good news is that in the Body of Christ all are needed. No one's reward will diminish the rewards of others. "Now the body is not made up of one part but of many. . . . The eye cannot say to the hand, 'I don't need you!' And the head cannot say to the feet, 'I don't need you!' On the contrary, those parts of the body that seem to be weaker are indispensable" (1 Corinthians 12:14, 21-22).

The fact that all are indispensable requires early and repeated proclamation to our children.

THE DEFINITION OF MANHOOD

During his comeback fight in *Rocky III*, the ex-champ slouched in his corner between rounds. Up to that point he had been pounded by the defending champion. Rocky's manager had a message for his dejected fighter: "He's just a man; be more than a man." Rocky proved his manhood by overcoming age, the odds, and his opponent. But biblical manhood has nothing to do with winning athletic contests. A man is one who is "temperate, worthy of respect, self-controlled, and sound in faith, in love and in endurance" (Titus 2:2). Our sons must be reminded that sports success can never establish their masculinity.

THE NATURE OF REWARDS

Athletes' rewards often vaporize after retirement. Former pro basketball player George McGinnis came to this realization upon retirement: "There is a truth I now understand. When everything is said and done, all I will be is the answer to a trivia question."[3]

As a parent, I want my sons involved in a rigorous training program, but one that trains for eternal, not temporal, rewards. Paul discussed that type of commitment: "Do you not know that in a race all the runners run, but only one gets the prize? Run in such a way as to get the prize. Everyone who competes in the games goes into strict training. They do it to get a crown that will not last; but we do it to get a crown that will last forever" (1 Corinthians 9:24-25).

3. Woodrow Paige, Jr., "McGinnis, Out of NBA, Accepts the Truth," *Minneapolis Tribune*, 5 Dec. 1982.

KINGDOM VISIONS

I still dream about trying to make my high school basketball team. Time has bent the dream—lately I have become a man in his late thirties trying to disguise himself as an eighteen year old! But the theme is still identifiable. I am striving to be the star I always longed to be.

My reoccurring dream was nurtured by a weekly ritual during basketball season. On Friday evenings, a cousin and I arrived early at the gym. The sophomore game was fuel for our growing excitement. As the start of the varsity game approached, the small gym was packed and vibrating with fans. The fervor heightened as the team emerged from the dressing room to the band's blasting of the school song. The warm-up minutes passed grudgingly, even though I was entranced with the shooting and dribbling skills of the young men on the floor.

Finally, as the boys were called back to the bench, the crowd became eerily quiet, waiting to burst into a thundering ovation as the name of each starter was announced. As the teams took the floor, we were on our feet, clapping and shouting, "Go! Go! Go! Go!" During the game we screamed our encouragement to the team and faithfully rebuked erring officials. The energy generated by the game often kept us playing one-on-one basketball past midnight in my cousin's driveway. Those evenings cradled a dream that is still alive in my subconsciousnes.

Childhood dreams are powerful. Vinny Testaverde, the 1986 winner of the Heisman Trophy (given to the individual who is voted the best college football player in the country), said that he had dreamed since boyhood that he would win the Heisman. Another athlete explained why he pursued a football career after being cut by his fourth team: "It's the Peter Pan complex. It's a desire not to grow up. It's like living in never-never land, playing the same game at 31 or 32 you were playing when you were 8."[4]

But we do not want our children to invest their hearts and souls in "never-never land." We want them to develop a vision of serving the King of kings. That will only take place if we expose them to models of that commitment.

But today kids have a neophyte knowledge of adult life. "In our specialized society, a child often has very little knowledge of his father's work. The extent of first-hand knowledge is that the father leaves home at an appointed hour, about the time that the child goes to school, five days a week. Beyond that, everything is hearsay."[5]

If we want our children to capture a vision of serving God, then we will have to expose them to a vision that incorporates the following principles.

CLEAR

Fourteen-year-old Robby Unser is receiving a "perfect" example of how to invest his life. His father and his uncle have both won the Indianapolis 500 three times. One of his uncles was killed while training for the race, and another was killed in the race itself. Young Robby has "been racing go-karts since age seven, sleeps in a bed shaped like a racing car, and his bedroom is cluttered with his father's and uncles' trophies as well as a healthy collection of his own."[6] Robby is immersed in a family dream.

4. Bob Abel and Mike Valenti, *Sports Quotes: The Inside View of the Sports World* (New York: Facts on File, 1983), p. 132.
5. Arnold Beisser, *The Madness in Sports* (New York: Appleton-Century-Crofts, 1967), p. 14.
6. Emily Greenspan, *Little Winners: Inside the World of the Child Sports Star* (Boston: Little, Brown, 1983), p. 52.

Jesus told us to uncover our lights for all to see—and that applies especially to our children. All the Bible lessons, all the memorized Scripture, and all the vacation Bible schools will not substitute for living models of the truth. Parents, we need to be creative. Take a family vacation to the mission field. Find Christians who will allow your child to apprentice during the summer. Invite mature believers into your home for a meal. Somehow get your child the exposure to individuals who model a commitment to serving the kingdom.

COMPELLING

When I was ten and my was cousin thirteen, we went with my family to Chicago, where we attended our first major league baseball game. I had watched games on TV, but the cameras edited out of the richness of a ballpark. I was awed by Wrigley Field: the grass was lush and perfectly clipped; the outfield walls were covered with an emerald-green ivy; the infield was smooth and finely textured, unlike the rock-infested diamond I played on; the foul lines were the whitest and straightest I had seen. I treasured the sounds—the loud popping of the catcher's mitt, the ear-splitting crack of the bat, the bellowing of the home plate umpire, the bartering calls of food vendors: "Get your red-hot hot dogs!" I marveled at the infielders' handling of "routine" grounders. I was astonished at the rocketing fly balls that were caught. I scrambled after fouls, hoping to retrieve a genuine, major league ball. That afternoon fostered a desire to play professional baseball.

What other professions have such compelling models for youth today? Very few. Dr. Paul Brand related the story of a surgical student who was paralyzed below the waist and scarred facially in a car crash. When she finished her training, she had a powerful ministry to lepers. Brand explained: "Dejected leprosy patients would loiter aimlessly in the hallways of their wards. Suddenly they would hear a small squeak that signified the approach of Mary's wheelchair. At once the row of faces lit up in bright smiles as though someone had just pronounced them all cured. Mary had a power to renew their faith and hope."[7] Why? Because they could see God alive in someone who, like them, had great physical deficiencies.

Proverbs tells us that "where there is no vision, the people perish" (Proverbs 29:18, KJV*). As parents we need to expose our children to compelling models of what it means to serve the Lord of the universe.

COMPLETE

One college football program instructs its men to invest their time in football and studies. Coach Frank Carver, former football coach at the University of Pittsburgh, was probably more honest about his athlete's commitments: "You don't go to bowl games with pre-med students."[8]

Occasionally, a young athlete will find someone in the sportsworld who has a more complete view of peoples' needs. Larry King attributes his high school coach —who took academics seriously—with guiding him toward writing. One day in class, Coach Noon got nothing but giggles in response to reading poetry. After class, King said Noon approached him with his voice trembling and said, "Smith can sit . . . in ignorance if he chooses, because he'll inherit a big ranch. Green is the son of a rich

*King James Version.
7. Paul Brand and Philip Yancey, *In His Image* (Grand Rapids: Zondervan, 1984), p. 42.
8. Abel and Valenti, p. 105.

oilman who'll take care of him. . . . But your father
. . . is a working man just like mine. If you expect to
amount to anything, you'll have to do it on your own."
King described his former coach and teacher as "a man
who did not waste his life nor permit me to entirely waste
mine."[9] If our children confine themselves to sports, they
will waste at least part of their potential.

The absence of adults as role models has left children
with a fuzzy view of the adult world. But the sportsworld
has been an exception to the diminution of adults: "A boy
will have daily encounters with sportsmen at all stages of
his development. Older brothers, coaches, fathers, and
fans are all eager to show him how the game is played."[10]
If we want our children to capture the vision of serving
the living God, then they must see that vision in action.

CONCLUSION

Parents are concerned about who their children are
becoming (their values) and what their children will do
with their lives (their visions). The following chapter provides practical advice for passing on biblical values and
visions to sports-involved children.

9. Larry King, "A Coach I Can't Forget," *Parade Magazine* (17 July 1983): 5.
10. Beisser, p. 14.

10

Passing on the Faith

An unruly child was asked to sit in the corner. He was insistent that he was going to accept the punishment *his* way. He wasn't going to sit in the corner; he was going to *stand* in the corner. His parent explained that that wasn't acceptable. The child acquiesced, but as he sat down he fumed, "I may be sitting down on the outside, but I'm standing up on the inside!"

Though a group of Christian youth may appear similarly committed, their behavior may not be indicative of their actual attitudes. Therefore, the goal of our instruction is not to make kids go to church or to have them memorize Scripture or to have them attend a Christian college—as important as those things may be. Our principal concern is the development of a heart commitment to biblical values.

Moses gave instruction in how that can take place:

> Hear, O Israel: The Lord our God, the Lord is one. Love the Lord your God with all your heart and with all your

soul and with all your strength. These commandments
that I give you today are to be upon your hearts. Im-
press them on your children. Talk about them when
you sit at home and when you walk along the road,
when you lie down and when you get up. Tie them as
symbols on your hands and bind them on your fore-
heads. Write them on the doorframes of your houses
and on your gates. (Deuteronomy 6:4-9)

Those instructions reveal two ways to communicate
truth to your children—by your walk (modeling) and
your talk (teaching). "Love the Lord *your* God with all
your heart and with all *your* soul and with all *your*
strength. These commandments . . . are to be on *your*
hearts" (emphasis added). Parent, Christian values will
seldom be adopted by your child unless you model those
values first. But action becomes complete when it is wed-
ded with speech. Teaching can be formal—"when you sit
at home"—or informal—"when you walk along the
road." The challenge is to impart truth to our sports-involved children.

MODELING

New York Yankee Yogi Berra became a coach after
his retirement from baseball. One day he was trying to
explain to a player how he could improve his hitting. As
Berra talked he became frustrated, realizing he wasn't
getting his point across. He grabbed the bat and said,
"Ah, just watch me do it." That is the essence of modeling—learning through observation.

Several studies have indicated that modeling is more
effective than preaching.[1] Whether modeling is *more* im-

---

1. Peter Fehrenbach, David Miller, and Mark Thelen, "The Importance of Consistency of Modeling Behavior upon Imitation," *Journal of Personality and
   Social Psychology* 37, no. 8 (1979): 1416.

portant is not the issue. What is important is that a parent must be the person he wants his child to become.

PARENTS AS MODELS

Not all modeled behavior is mirrored. Just because you go to church doesn't mean your child will go when he is an adult. Just because you are generous doesn't mean that your child will be generous. What determines a model's effectiveness?

First, children are more likely to copy the behavior of a consistent model. We are to love God with *all* our hearts, minds, and souls. Our Christian commitment must affect our children more than our church attendance or our vocabulary.

One day I asked my sons to tape a championship game on our video recorder while I had another commitment. Because I enjoy the unexpected in sports, I made clear that I wanted to view the game without knowing the final score. When I got home, my middle son, who was six years old at the time, solemnly recommended that I not watch the game. I immediately knew that my team had lost. I began to boil. "Oh, Andrew. You weren't supposed to tell me!" Unfortunately, my values were showing. I was more concerned about the football game than the feelings of my son. As sports journalist Glenn Dickey points out, the real problem with an overemphasis on sports is parents:

> The real problem is that athletes are idolized at least as much by adults as kids. It is not kids who make up booster clubs; it is not kids who buy season tickets; it is not kids who wait at airports to greet athletes returning from a trip; it is not kids who buy lawn mowers be

cause Jack Nicklaus (who probably hasn't used one in 15 years) says one brand is the best.[2]

One study found that 60 percent of men and 40 percent of women talk frequently or very frequently about sports. You may tell your child, for example, that an education is more important than being successful in athletics, but what do your actions communicate? Do you read with your child? Do you tell him what you are learning? Do you follow up a question about beetles with a trip to the library? If you want your child to value such things as an inquisitive mind, then you must model that priority.

The second factor that governs the modeling of behavior is whether those actions are rewarded or punished. In one study, children observed an adult acting aggressively toward a large doll. Some children then observed the adult being rewarded, others saw the adult punished, and others saw the adult receive no reward or punishment. The children were then given solitary time with the doll. Those who saw the adult rewarded for aggression treated the doll with much greater hostility.

God's order also distributes rewards and punishments: "Do not be deceived: God cannot be mocked. A man reaps what he sows. The one who sows to please his sinful nature, from that nature will reap destruction; the one who sows to please the Spirit, from the Spirit will reap eternal life" (Galatians 6:7-8).

Therefore, the principle of modeling implies that kids do not have to be—and probably shouldn't be—shielded from all the sins of their parents and other adults. When they see the "rewards" of sin, they will not be tempted to copy such behavior.

Because of the visibility of sportsworld models,

2. Glenn Dickey, *Jock Empire* (Radnor, Pa.: Chilton, 1974), p. 208.

many parents are rightfully concerned about their influence. When the *Washington Star* ran a series of articles on homosexuality in sports, they received a flood of mail. One man's response was typical: "Kids today will hesitate to admit wanting to be soldiers (murderers), federal agents or policemen (burglars), blue-collar workers (unemployed), small businessmen (broke), doctors (sued) or President (crook). Thanks for messing with the image of the pro athlete."[3]

But what is the impact of such articles? Are present-day revelations of drug involvement, gambling, and sexual deviance bad for kids?

ATHLETES AS MODELS

After the 1983 baseball season, Kansas City was shocked to discover that some of the leading players on the Royals' team had been using illegal drugs. (Since then, such revelations have become commonplace.) The team's management held town meetings in which other team members talked to the fans about the drug problems. John Wathan, a catcher for the Royals, explained the fans' attitude: "People are angry, and I don't blame them. They're upset because baseball players are supposed to be role models for their children."[4] Yes, athletes do act as role models for children. Yes, parents should be concerned about their behavior. But some of our concerns seem misplaced.

First, God is concerned about those who have a greater influence on children than sports heroes—parents! Hall of Fame pitcher Bob Gibson became tired of the pressure to be a good example and exhorted parents,

3. Neil Isaacs, *Jock Culture, U.S.A.* (New York: Norton, 1978), p. 46.
4. Erik Brady, "Royals Fall from Grace," *USA Today*, 18 Nov. 1983.

"Why do I have to be an example for your kid? You be an example for your kid."[5] Good advice.

Second, in attempting to give children good role models, parents, athletes, team owners, commissioners, and the media have often collaborated in presenting a distorted view of sports. It is now well-known that Babe Ruth was not the saint that he was portrayed to be. He was a heavy drinker and a glutton. He contracted a venereal disease. He lost huge sums of money gambling. And he was constantly in trouble with the league's president for his misbehaviors.

But why is *"fakelore,"* as Jim Bouton describes it, created? Some believe it is necessary to shield children from the fact that some of their athletic heroes are really contemptible. But is that true?

Not every childhood model must be sweet and innocent. The Bible does not edit out sin, even among its heroes. Abraham was prepared to sacrifice his wife to save his life. Joseph was a spoiled, egotistical brat. Moses killed a man. Samson was a fornicator. David was an adulterer and a murderer. The Bible presents both good and bad. God knows that we learn from both. So why do we become dismayed when a professing Christian dies of an overdose of drugs? It is a powerful reminder of the wages of sin.

When the sportsworld constructs "fakelore" it stresses the *appearance* of goodness rather than goodness itself. The Baltimore Colts had first pick in the 1983 NFL draft and chose quarterback John Elway. When Elway was adamant about not playing in Baltimore, Colts owner Robert Irsay reluctantly traded him. But it wasn't a dead issue for Irsay: "We signed up a couple of boys this week who are looking for Elway. . . . We are going to get

5. Bob Abel and Mike Valenti, *Sports Quotes: The Inside View of the Sports World* (New York: Facts on File, 1983), p. 122.

Elway." But just one day later Irsay—after a reprimand from the NFL commissioner—retracted those statements. "What reference we made is that several of our defensive players, without mentioning their names, are quarterback sackers. If Elway's a quarterback, they would go after him, just like any other quarterback. That is the intent of the entire statement."[6]

But when an NFL owner's angry words are not whitewashed, it opens a window to life's realities. Think about the issues that a parent and child could discuss:

• Is it natural to feel hurt—as Irsay was—when we sense rejection?
• How do you think the other players may have felt about Elway's wishes?
• How might the problem be solved?
• Did Elway have a right to play where he wished?

That instance could have been an excellent opportunity to talk about the source and the resolution of conflicts.

Furthermore, performing plastic surgery on sports' ills may increase sports' allure. If we want to nurture realistic dreams in our children, then the fairy-tale view of sports must be laid bare.

ATHLETES AND HEROES

Children do not have any great visions because they have no great heroes. They are yearning to be "wildly famous, androgynous, and good at climbing walls."[7] Children need genuine heroes to stir their hearts and imaginations (cf. Hebrews 11). But the answer is not to try to

6. "Irsay Says Colts Will 'Get' Elway," *Sioux Falls Argus Leader,* 7 May 1983.
7. Ralph Schoenstein, "The Modern Mount Rushmore," *Newsweek* 104, no. 6 (6 Aug. 1984): 82.

make heroes out of non-heroes. Journalist Robert Lipsyte was upset with his fellow sports writers who were "shedding tears for the knees of Namath and all our crippled heroes playing through agony to teach us courage." He explained his own feelings: "What a cruel joke. That season Jacqueline Susann and Cornelius Ryan were writing through agony for us, dying of cancer. And sports writers were defining success, failure, manhood, femininity, cowardice, and courage on the actions of athletes."[8]

We have trouble finding genuine heroes because we are searching in such a small area. The world is filled with authentic heroes to kindle our children's dreams. The Landmark book series for children has more than one hundred biographies of famous men and women who have had remarkable impacts on world history. There may be an elderly, arthritic woman in your church whose joyous countenance is an inversion of her chronic pain. There may be a gifted teacher who has given up higher paying jobs because of his concern for children. Help your children get to know those legitimate heroes.

TEACHING

Children need more than examples. The truth must be explained and applied in the midst of their daily lives —"when you sit at home, when you walk along the road, when you lie down and when you get up." We talk about giving our children quality time as though "life could be dehydrated and concentrated to avoid the dull spots." But many of the choicest opportunities arise when we spend chunks of time with our children. Recently my wife was transporting our son and two of his friends to a ball game. One friend thoughtlessly berated the skills of the

8. Robert Lipsyte, *Sportsworld: An American Dreamland* (New York: Quadrangle, 1975), p. 63.

other friend. When we got home we were able to discuss with our son the insensitivity of his friend. We reminded him that Proverbs admonishes us to wound our friends when necessary. A Sunday school lesson a week later may have been too late. Many opportunities come unexpectedly when we are together.

FORMAL INSTRUCTION

Formal instruction should not be equated with a three-hour lecture! "Formal" simply means planning such things as the content, place, and time. Taking a child to church or to a lecture, discussing a book, and having family worship are all examples of formal instruction. How can you use those types of instruction to communicate biblical truth to your children?

Commitment to the message. Formal instruction is most effective when the listener makes a commitment to the message. When Jesus selected the twelve, He asked them to commit themselves to an itinerant ministry. Later, He sent them out to minister in the cities.

Consider again Muzafer Sherif's tests on the effects of prolonged competition upon two rival groups at a boys' camp. The competition kindled deep animosities that resisted removal. Verbal appeals through religious services had little effect. Sherif explained what finally worked:

> The goals that were effective were problem situations —an apparent breakdown in the water system at a time when outside help was not immediately available; how to get another movie when the camp was short on funds and neither group had enough canteen funds left to sponsor a movie alone; a stalled Mack truck that was the sole vehicle to go for food when everyone was hungry and which was far too large for one group to

push or pull alone; food preparation at a time when everyone was very hungry even though "separate but equal" facilities were available but less efficient; tent pitching when all were tired and when the poles and stakes had somehow gotten all mixed up.[9]

The hostility disappeared only after a series of such engineered crises. An occasional Bible lesson has little impact. But when God's Word is recurrently applied to the daily lives of children it is very effective.

What types of actions encourage biblical values in our sports-involved children? If your child is skilled in a sport, he might practice with a less-skilled teammate. An older child can learn how to care for others by coaching a younger group of children. Your child can develop independence by earning money to pay for special sports equipment. Biblical values will never be passed on unless you ask your child to make concrete commitments to them.

INFORMAL INSTRUCTION

When a mother becomes tense and fearful with predictions of severe storms, she is engaging in informal instruction. She doesn't prepare a lesson entitled "The Fearful Threat of Storms." Nevertheless, she lucidly communicates that lesson by a tense voice, nervous attention to weather news, and frequent statements about the threat of storms. Informal instruction may be the way that most values are learned. Our challenge is to control and interpret those subtle influences for our children.

The child's environment. The Chinese leaders are the

9. Muzafer Sherif, "The Social Context of Competition," in *Joy and Sadness in Children's Sport*, ed. Rainer Martens (Champaign, Ill.: Human Kinetics, 1978), p. 96.

architects of their culture. Dr. Terry Orlick explained their methods:

> Almost everything in China has some educational pur-
> pose. [The message of cooperation] comes through
> comic books, children's books, children's plays, puppet
> shows, feature and documentary films, theatre, music,
> exhibitions, art, sculpture, woodcuts, pictures, posters,
> stamps, billboards, dances, songs, physical culture,
> school, industrial work, agricultural work, historical
> sites, ballets, and even the circus.[10]

You can control your child's environment. As you thoughtfully reward certain behavior, you build an atmosphere that will bend your child toward biblical values. When my oldest son reads a book to my youngest, I can say, "Wow, you're a great brother!" Or when one shares a toy, I can wrap my arms around him, telling him how enthused Jesus and I are about his generosity.

But many influences are beyond our control. In such cases, our kids need help interpreting those "backdoor" messages. When high school students adulate athletes, when a child is ridiculed for his clumsiness, or when a TV announcer glorifies professional sports, assistance is needed in evaluating such events.

Television has become a primary means of transmitting sports values. If you watch televised sports with your child—and if he does you should—it is important that you understand the dangers and opportunities associated with it.

Televised sports and informal instruction. In a three-hour televised event, an announcer speaks more than

10. Terry Orlick, *Winning Through Cooperation* (Washington, D.C.: Acropolis, 1978), p. 63.

25,000 words—an equivalent of 60 written pages.[11] Applying that formula to the 1984 Summer Olympics, the words of ABC's announcers could fill a book 3,600 pages long! But what impact does that flood of words have on the millions who watch?

Biased reporting. TV is entertainment, and broadcasters pay hundreds of millions of dollars yearly for the rights to televise sports. They in turn sell time to advertisers. The result of that arrangement is that TV covers sports "more flamboyantly than honestly." In order to attract viewers, "The Game of the Week has to be transmitted as the Game of the Decade. It's in the contract; advertisers simply don't sponsor dull games."[12]

The marketing of sports is built on the illusion that the results matter. When the American hockey team defeated the Soviets in the 1980 Olympics, Americans went wild.

> But realistically speaking, why should it have made any difference at all? We can easily see why the result makes a difference to those playing, those running the business, those connected with some ancillary business, and their families. And it's easy to see why the outcome matters to anyone who makes a large bet. But the hockey game had absolutely no real-world influence on relations between the US and the USSR, on the arms race, on what was happening in Afghanistan.[13]

Like the American hockey fans, we are included among the deceived. We tune in as if our eternal destinies were at stake. Controversial Dallas Cowboy running back

11. Leonard Koppett, *Sports Illusion, Sports Reality: A Reporter's View of Sports, Journalism, and Society* (Boston: Houghton Mifflin, 1981), p. 138.
12. Abel and Valenti, p. 211.
13. Koppett, p. 12.

Duane Thomas may have been an enigma to his coach, teammates, and fans because he was able to keep sports in perspective. His response to the pre-Super-Bowl hype was: "If it was the ultimate game, they wouldn't be playing it again next year."[14]

The bias remains because leagues can fire announcers or withhold TV contracts. As a result,

> what announcer is going to suggest that the college draft . . . [is] probably unconstitutional? Or that the rule forbidding college athletes to have agents is unfair? . . . Or that scholarships should go to underprivileged scholars and not athletes? In short, who is questioning the basic values of college and professional sports? Not anybody you're likely to see on network television.[15]

Watching televised sports. Some parents have chosen to discard their sets, believing that all TV is harmful. Though that could be a wise course for some, what about the rest of us weaker-willed souls?

First, since kids need assistance in interpreting their world, it is critical to watch sports with them. In 1982 my sons and I watched the finals of the NCAA basketball tournament. The game was decided in the final seconds when a Georgetown player mistakenly threw the ball to an opponent. At the end of the game, a teammate put his arms around the erring player. Later, I asked my sons which player I would have been most proud to call my son. They were unsure. I said that it wasn't the highest scorer or one of the winners or the best defender. It was

14. Roger Staubach, *Time Enough to Win* (Waco, Tex.: Word, 1980), p. 99.
15. Jim Bouton, *Ball Four* (Briarcliff Manor, N.Y.: Stein & Day, 1981), p. 412.

the one who graciously forgave his teammate. There is both good and bad, truth and hype—but kids need help in seeing the difference.

Second, as you view sports, remind yourself that the sun will still come up tomorrow, that water will continue to be wet, that Jesus will still be Lord of the universe regardless of who wins. By now you know that I was deeply entangled in the sportsworld. Results *did* matter. Games took precedence over people. But a strange thing happened when I reminded myself that results did not personally matter—my zeal subsided. It didn't happen all at once, but I now find that sports frequently bore me. Now I am more interested in a close game, excellent play, and good sportsmanship than in seeing my team win. That is the view of sports that I want my sons to have. For example, I demonstrate my interest in a close game by rooting for the team that is behind and even switching teams if the situation reverses!

Other viewing suggestions include not tuning in until an event is half over. If it is close then you can watch what is left. If not, you won't waste time. Also, try turning off the sound. The withdrawal may be difficult at first, but our family has come to enjoy the silence and the greater opportunity to talk.

CONCLUSION

Richard Lipsky remembered the influence of his father at track meets: "His whole world of meaning and triumph was re-created before his eyes, as well as mine. He would point out the different strides of the runners, talk excitedly about finishing kicks, and come alive—be happy—in ways I never otherwise saw. I could not have received a more vivid lesson about what was important in life."[16]

Frequently, your most enduring instructions are unplanned and unintentional. Mr. Lipsky did not plan the outing with the purpose of revealing his values. But he did. Does Jesus Christ make you "come alive"? Or do you show more enthusiasm when talking about a new car, making money, playing golf, or going shopping? If you are serious about the commitments of your child, you must first be concerned about your own commitments.

16. Richard Lipsky, *How We Play the Game* (Boston: Beacon, 1981), p. 66.

11

The Influence of the Church

Throughout the centuries God's people have frequently absorbed rather than transformed pagan culture. But what about sports? Are we the influencers or the influenced? Although Christian involvement in sports is flourishing with athletes' ministries, pastors serving as chaplains, Christian schools developing top athletic teams, and summer camps training athletes and coaches, our impact on sports appears minimal. The values of the sportsworld have seemingly become our values.

THE CONFORMED CHURCH

THE EMPHASIS ON WINNING

Christians sometimes seem as enamored with winning as the sportsworld. One Christian sports magazine asked football coach George Allen for his views on success. He has been known to state that an occasional fight with an opponent is good for team morale. He is the one who told his players, "The winner is the only individual who is truly alive."[1] (Jesus said we must lose life to find life.) But the article confronted none of his excesses. What are we doing when we include such a model in a Christian magazine for young athletes?

Some Christians justify an accent on winning by claiming that it gives them a megaphone to the world. Dave Hannah, the originator of the evangelistic sports teams for Campus Crusade, explained his view: "Who has better attendance—first-place or last-place teams? Who is featured in the newspapers more—the nation's finest or the also-rans? Who do people write about, talk about, pay to see? Winners!"[2] Am I suggesting that we try to lose? No. But if we overly stress winning, it may erode our priorities. If I coach at a Christian school and want to win as a testimony to our opponents, what priority does winning take? If it becomes too critical I may forget to help my players develop realistic goals for the future; I may come to view the athletic "mission" as the school's most important task; I may recruit athletes who make the program a winner but who do not reflect Christ's character. And I'm not saying that winning cannot be *a* goal, but it should not be the *only* goal.

ATHLETES' TESTIMONIALS

John McEnroe offers us clean shaves with Bic. Roger Staubach offers us relief with R-O-L-A-I-D-S. Arnold Palmer offers us help to keep the old equipment in shape with Pennzoil. So why shouldn't Christian athletes be used to "sell" Jesus? "If athletes endorse products, why

1. "George Allen on Success," *Athletes in Action* (Fall 1981): 19.
2. Joe Smalley, *More Than a Game* (San Bernardino, Calif.: Here's Life, 1981), p. 37.

can't they endorse a way of life? Athletes and coaches, be it right or wrong, have a platform in this country. Athletes have power, a voice. So, simply, how can we best use this for something constructive in the faith life?"[3]

This widely used practice sounds logical—but where is the biblical justification for using well-known Christians in such a way? Did the early church look for religious leaders, the wealthy, government officials, or other prominent people to proclaim the message? The apostle Paul would have been the ideal witness—by our way of thinking—to reach his fellow Jews. He had an appropriate pedigree. He had diplomas from the best Jewish seminaries. He was a member of the most respected religious organization and a zealous persecutor of the church. But when Paul opened his mouth before the Jews they wanted to kill him. Paul's ministry was eventually among Gentiles, where his breeding and accomplishments were meaningless.

Where do Christians in sports reflect the truth that "God chose the foolish things of the world to shame the wise; God chose the weak things of the world to shame the strong. He chose the lowly things of this world and the despised things —and the things that are not—to nullify the things that are, so that no one may boast before him"? Sometimes believers uphold the strong and beautiful, thereby putting down the weak and unlovely. My college fellowship used that strategy. We wanted to win leaders, believing that they would have the greatest impact on the school. We were confused. God's strategy is different. He wants to take nobodies and make somebodies out of them.

3. D. Edmond Hiebert, *Prevailing Protestant Ideology Concerning Sport* (Otterburne, Manitoba: Winnepeg Bible College, 1981), p. 184.

The clamor to use athletes in spreading the gospel can also abuse athletes. We focus on using their testimony rather than on building their walk with God.

Futhermore, many Christian athletes are better ambassadors for the athletic dream than for Jesus. When they come to town they are asked and often talk more about their athletic careers than about their walk with Christ. Kids may be more inclined to follow the unrealistic dream of professional sports than a closer walk with God.

Finally, the use of such testimonials may subvert the role of sports. When athletics becomes a means to an end (i.e., reaching the world), its genuine purposes—exercise, fun, and friendships—may be lost.

Are Christians attempting to make sports more readily available for the elderly or the handicapped? Why are there no Christian organizations dedicated to training volunteer coaches for the benefit of the millions of participants? Why aren't Christians dedicated to developing new or better forms of sports? A lack of Christian involvement in those areas shows that we have forgotten that sports can be enjoyed soley for what they are.

THE "TOTAL" ATHLETE

Some Christian athletes seem to believe that anything less than total involvement in sports discredits their witness for Christ. Dedication is important, but its focus must not be too narrow.

Kyle Rote, Jr., appears to be a healthy exception to such a contracted view. In the midst of a successful soccer career he decided to take a sabbatical. His primary reasons were to spend more time with his family: "You can't exercise on Saturday and let that carry you the rest of the week. You can't just visit with your family on Saturday.

There has to be almost daily interaction with the family."

He also sees the value of getting firsthand exposure to world problems: "I'm not on any one-man crusade to save all the hungry people in world. I just want to add what I can to the ongoing programs and to get beyond the stage of sitting in my house and sending out token checks, trying to make myself feel good."[4]

A corollary to the give-God-everything advice is the idea that any athletic talent should be developed to its fullest: "Your athletic abilities have been given to you by God. . . . You have more than some athletes and less than others. But you do have at least one talent's worth of athletic abilities. God expects you to invest wisely the talents you do have."[5]

If I practiced more, I could probably be a top amateur golfer. Am I, therefore, required to hone that talent? I don't think so. God has more important tasks for me.

But quitting is often viewed as anathema. Wes Neal said, "There is nothing wrong with desiring to quit. Every athlete has within him that desire when the going gets extremely difficult. . . . How you handle that desire determines if you are a winner from God's viewpoint."[6]

But our children should know that quitting can be a mature response under certain conditions.

THE TRANSFORMED CHURCH

THE ROLE OF CHRISTIANS

The early church sought to correct the abuse of sports while upholding the value of physical exercise. Ralph Ballou said the church Fathers believed that evil

4. John Carvalho, "Kyle Takes a Time-out," *Athletes in Action* (Fall 1980): 43.
5. Wes Neal, *Athletic Perfection* (Milford, Mich.: Mott Media, 1981), p. 48.
6. Ibid., p. 80.

was "neither inherent in man nor in [physical] activity."[7] Their concern was for the way sport was conducted—as ours should be today.

Of all the present-day abuses, the most serious may be the worship of sports. The transformed church can mirror the only legitimate alternative to the adulation of sport.

THE WORSHIP OF SPORTS

There were 2,000 journalists at the Geneva Summit Conference—but 2,400 at Super Bowl XX. A president admitted that he read the sports section first. When high school students were asked how they would like to be remembered, the majority said as an athlete.

Sports have become almost a cult. Why such reverence? The answer may be found in history. As the Roman culture deteriorated, sports became increasingly important. Our culture may be showing similar signs. God has created us for worship. If we do not worship Him, we will turn to false gods—materialism, sensuality, power, and even sports. One football player at the University of Texas recalled being a part of "an immense tradition [i.e., Longhorn football] where winning football games is a sacrament of such emotional intensity as to rival those of any other religion."[8]

Sports, as religion, can feed people's need for transcendence, significance, community, and coherence.

7. Ralph Ballou, "An Analysis of the Writings of Selected Church Fathers," in *The History of Sport and Physical Education to 1900*, ed. E. Ziegler (Champaign, Ill.: Stripes, 1973), p. 196.
8. Gary Shaw, *Meat on the Hoof: The Hidden World of Texas Football* (New York: St. Martin, 1972), p. ix.

Transcendence. A former NFL quarterback, Gary Cuozzo, discussed the emotional impact of performing in packed stadiums:

> Several years ago I returned to Baltimore for an old-timers' reunion. I cannot describe the feeling when I walked on that field and felt the sixty-five thousand people surrounding me, heard their noise, anticipated the whistle for the kickoff. I started to quiver. . . . I had goose bumps. . . . I wanted to cry. You must have competed at that level to know what it's like. It was an eerie, other-worldly experience.[9]

But such an experience is not confined to the participants. I shared similar feelings when sitting in the stands at high school basketball, Minnesota Twins baseball, and SMU football games. Such sports experiences evidence a need for transcendence, the need to feel a part of something grander than ourselves.

When my wife and I were in college we spent a week at a conference with more than five hundred other Christians. We were new to the faith and part of a small group of believers on a campus that was mostly hostile to our faith. At that time, neither of us wanted our commitments widely known. But that conference transformed us. I don't fully understand the cause, but the effect was a greater boldness and confidence in our faith. When Paul wrote to the Colossians he informed them, "All over the world this gospel is producing fruit and growing, just as it has been doing among you" (Colossians 1:6). Transcendent feelings were stirred when we recognized the breadth of God's work.

9. Gary Warner, *Competition* (Elgin, Ill.: David C. Cook, 1979), p. 244.

But such religious experiences are infrequent for most people, who look elsewhere to meet the need: "It has been a relatively easy transition for many Americans from the ritual of Sunday worship in church to the ritual of the Sunday game of the week on television."[10] Or, as one retired athlete said, "[No other work] sweeps you away into a different world. Sports is close to religion for me. It has its own spiritual beauty."[11] We all have a need to be swept away into something beyond ourselves. Only the worship of God will wholly satisfy that need.

Significance. We feel significant when we successfully complete a task. John Naber achieved his goal of winning four gold medals at the 1976 Olympics. He explained the feeling: "Basically, it was the fulfillment of all the hours I had spent. It occurred to me that this was just like taking the last step to the top of Mount Everest."[12]

But even for those few who climb the mountain, sports achievement cannot wholly satisfy. Jim Bouton explained:

> Somehow my past successes hadn't made me feel secure. There were all these thoughts racing through my mind, fragments of this and that. It was like listening to twelve radio stations at the same time. And I had trouble breathing. Sometimes I'd get this tightness in my chest and it felt as if I was buried ten feet underground breathing through a straw, terrified that someone would kick dirt into it. The illusion was always that it

10. Arnold Beisser, *The Madness in Sports* (New York: Appleton-Century-Crofts, 1967), p. 142.
11. Ed Kiersh, *Where Have You Gone Vince Dimaggio?* (New York: Bantam, 1983), p. 235.
12. Rick Arndt, *Winning with Christ* (St. Louis: Concordia, 1982), p. 50.

would come with the next achievement, the next success. If I could just find that ultimate accomplishment I'd be safe.[13]

When initial sports success doesn't satisfy, we seek greater achievements. It's like trying to extinguish a headache. If two aspirins don't ease the pain, maybe two more will. It never occurs to us that we may be using the wrong medicine.

But there is a remedy that satisfies. Paul explained: "So then, men ought to regard us as servants of Christ and as those entrusted with the secret things of God. Now it is required that those who have been given a trust must prove faithful" (1 Corinthians 4:1-2).

Whether a person is a dentist, a bricklayer, a salesman, a secretary, or an athlete, his significance is found in responding daily to the will of his heavenly Father. The athlete who tries to build his self-worth through what happens in sports will find that he is depending on "broken cisterns that cannot hold water" (Jeremiah 2:13).

Community. Religious traditions serve to bind people together. Formerly, religious festivals "marked the seasons of the year; a child was baptized, confirmed, and later married and buried" at special church celebrations. Those events brought "the community together to reaffirm its common purpose, common origins, and common beliefs."[14]

With religious experience waning, people look elsewhere for community. Journalist Blaine Johnson explained how sports teams have filled this need: "The longing of people to belong to something cannot be over-

13. Jim Bouton, *Ball Four* (Briarcliff Manor, N.Y.: Stein & Day, 1981), p. 422.
14. Beisser, p. 141.

rated. Mobility and expansion have fragmented the sense of community for most people and the local sports teams are the strongest magnet available to give one a sense of belonging, of being 'in this thing together.' "[15]

The director of a Los Angeles mission for the homeless explained what happened when the Olympic committee donated a TV and made it an official watching spot: "These men are close to being completely alone. It's wonderful how this has brought them together."[16]

Whether it is the USA Olympic team, a child's Little League team, the city's professional team, or the local high school team, sports act as a communal glue. Parents get to know one another. Social and economic barriers are bridged on the field and in the stands. It gives the town something to talk about that does not involve widely differing viewpoints.

But what kind of cohesiveness does it offer? Isn't it more of a respite than a resolution? The superficial basis of unity (i.e., the team and its welfare) does not cure the loneliness of the homeless; it does not bring students and teachers together to solve important educational problems; it has little impact upon the prejudices that alienate the races; it cannot solve the problems that divide cities.

The Jew-Gentile conflict during the time of Jesus was as deep as any Arab-Jew or black-white conflict today. But in the early church Jews and Gentiles ate together, ministered together, worshiped together. Paul explained the source of that unity: "[Christ Jesus] is our peace, who has made the two one and has destroyed the barrier, the

15. Blaine Johnson, *What's Happenin'?* (Englewood Cliffs, N.J.: Prentice-Hall, 1978), p. 122.
16. Pete Axthelm, "L.A. Is as Good as Gold," *Newsweek*, 104, no. 7 (13 Aug. 1984): 29.

dividing wall of hostility" (Ephesians 2:14). Jesus said the world will recognize that He was sent by the Father when Christians display that type of unity. Our job is not simply to criticize the idolatry of the world but to show them that worshiping the true God fulfills their deepest longing.

Coherence. We live in a complex world in which even the problems are unclear. What ails marriage, with its near 50 percent breakup rate? What plagues our economy—an unbalanced budget? governmental control? Are we aiding despots or Communism in Central America? Is the Soviet Union a genuine threat, and if so, how should we defend ourselves? What are the causes and cures of world hunger? Life's problems are baffling. But sports share none of those ambiguities, as political columnist James Reston pointed out when discussing the near conclusion of the 1979 World Series between Baltimore and Pittsburgh.

> The hits and errors will be clear, and the heroes and goats will be identified. In sports, if not in politics, there are clear rules, boundaries, foul-lines, endlines, goal lines, and referees or umpires to decide by instant decisions or instant replays what really happened. This gives a certain security to the scene. No wonder, then, that when everything else is uncertain and confused, it is easier and more popular to concentrate and choose up sides between the Pirates and Orioles.[17]

But Christians do not have to escape to the comforting coherence of the sportsworld. We have a Lord who

17. Leonard Koppett, *Sports Illusion, Sports Reality: A Reporter's View of Sports, Journalism, and Society* (Boston: Houghton Mifflin, 1981), p. 20.

provides us with "more and more knowledge and
. . . depth of insight, so that [we] may be able to discern
what is best" (Philippians 1:9). Even in areas where our
understanding is incomplete, we can confidently say:
"Even though I walk through the valley of the shadow of
death, I will fear no evil, for you are with me; your rod
and your staff, they comfort me" (Psalm 23:4).

At one time I was trapped in the seductive web of the
sportsworld. (And like an alcoholic, I must be careful lest
I become entangled again.) Sports captured my whole being. I analyzed sports news as carefully as any scholar
ever studied the Bible. It may be hard for some to understand such devotion. But I am not unique; worshiping
sports is not an uncommon problem.

Richard Lipsky allowed sports to dominate his life
when his personal life was in turmoil. His immersion into
the New York Knicks basketball team game him the fellowship he desperately needed: "My season ticket gave
me entry into a Madison Square Garden revival meeting.
. . . As the Garden became a place of worship, the sports
pages of the New York Post became holy writ. [The sports
journalists] fueled the devotional spirit. Fans read about
the dramatic confrontation before entering that night's
contest."

The Knicks, who were perennial non-contenders,
found themselves fighting for the championship that
year. Lipsky explained the effect on the fans: "A warm
camaraderie built as the Knicks began to redeem us from
our years of suffering." Fans celebrated exceptional plays
by leaping out of their seats and slapping each other's
hands.

The Knicks made it to the championship series, but
during the fifth game their star Willis Reed was injured.
The team's hopes pinned on his ability to play in the final
game. When the warm-ups began Reed was not on the

floor. The fans nervously watched the players' entryway. When Reed appeared Lipsky said he felt "the same feeling I used to get as a kid when the cavalry appeared on the hill to rescue the helpless settlers." Fans and players alike joyously embraced.

When the Knicks won that night, Lipsky explained that it was the emotional peak of his life:

> I was soaking wet. I yelled out the window. My suffering had been redeemed. I felt as if no one could ever understand my feelings at that moment. . . . Ever since I had been a 5'1" seventh-grader, I had dreamed of being a Knick. I had practiced for hours, six and seven days a week. I was a good player, . . but I was never going to be a Knick. Yet somehow at that moment I was a Knick. I had given the team and the game of basketball a huge chunk of my emotional life, and I was repaid in this moment of mystical communion.[18]

But sports are not "the living water." They may temporarily refresh, but they will demand repeated trips to the well.

CONCLUSION

Since sports are "changing the course of childhood," it is my hope that you will begin your own analysis of sports. For many of us, the investigation should begin by delving into our own passion for sports.

Are we glued to Sunday afternoon football? Are we more exuberant over a high school football game than a home Bible study? Do we prod our children to excel in sports while giving token encouragement to other skills?

18. Richard Lipsky, *How We Play the Game* (Boston: Beacon, 1981), pp. 35-38.

Do we spend more time with the sports page than with our Bibles?

Sports, as all of God's gifts, may be used or abused. When used properly, sports can enhance a child's physical, emotional, and spiritual development. When abused, it can have an enduring negative impact on children. Your attitude toward sports will be one of the primary factors in determining how sports will affect your children. May God give you wisdom in directing their involvement in sports.